THE SAN QUENTIN STORY

THE SAN QUENTIN STORY

BY WARDEN CLINTON T. DUFFY

AS TOLD TO DEAN JENNINGS

GREENWOOD PRESS, PUBLISHERS
NEW YORK   1968

FOR GLADYS: Without whose faith and love I could not have lived the San Quentin Story.

C. T. D.

INTRODUCTION: One evening not very long ago I went to the movies to see a prison picture. The film was advertised as a "shocker," and in many ways it was. I wanted to see it because I had heard that the locale, although disguised, was supposed to be San Quentin and that the story had been written by a man who had done time. I got quite an education that night. I saw a warden who was a pawn in the hands of a scheming chief guard. I saw that all the prisoners except the hero were cruel, moronic characters who shuffled around in sloppy clothes which had large black numbers stenciled on them. The men were busy day and night plotting all sorts of violence, and they talked from the sides of their mouths in some sort of underworld slang. I am sure that if the film had been in color the prison walls would have been the traditional "grim" gray. The guards were vicious and clubbed prisoners whenever they felt like it. Visitors talked to prisoners through glass and wire partitions while suspicious guards listened in. Before the film ended, virtually all the principals were wounded or dead, and under the circumstances that was probably a good thing.

I have no quarrel with the movie makers, since these misconceptions about prisons are widespread and persistent, and also are probably good box-office. I suspect that the public likes to think of penitentiaries as medieval forts bristling with guns and bursting with violence and death. In the past nine years I have opened the gates of San Quentin to thousands of visitors—I am being kidded more and more about the tours to "Duffy's tavern"—because people should see for themselves how life really is behind our walls. But you would be amazed how many of our visitors walk around the prison in fear, as though they were in a cage full of lions, and then are crestfallen, even a little resentful, if there are no incidents.

Somewhere there may be prisons like those I have seen on the screen. San Quentin itself in the old days was often a hell-on-earth, and even today, despite what all of us have tried to do, it is no summer resort. I have seen men who had been suddenly and mysteriously stabbed to death. I have already had to execute eighty-four men and two women. Twice I was nearly kidnaped by prisoners who might have killed me in order to break out. We have had our share of escapes and minor rebellions, and we fight a constant war against a small group of smugglers, counterfeiters, forgers, drug addicts, murderers, and thieves who commit crimes behind walls just as they did outside. There is even a daily reminder of these risks, if you can call them that, in my own home—a bullet embedded in the wall of a small reception room. The shot was fired by men who were trying to kill another warden some years ago, and it missed him by inches. I confess I have left the bullet deliberately—not so much as a warning to myself, but because it satisfies the morbid curiosity of some taxpaying visitors who might otherwise be disappointed in their penal system.

I also remember a group of Russians who came to San Quentin in 1945 while they were delegates to the first United Nations Conference in San Francisco. I can still see the puzzled expressions on their stolid faces as they were guided around, and finally, as they started out the gate, still intact, the leader shrugged and said stiffly: "This has been most interesting, Mr. Duffy—but *this* is not a prison." I know what he meant, and from the Russian viewpoint he was probably right. But while San Quentin is undeniably a prison, and one of the largest in the world at that, it is also a town. My home town, I like to think it is unlike any other town in the world because its heart is locked up; a town in exile that has had its face lifted, the scars of wild youth removed, the cruel wrinkles smoothed, the sagging jowls of spirit raised. A town beginning to live again.

Just the other day I happened to be at the main gate— it isn't really much of a gate, because any kid with a jalopy could knock it down—when an old-time burglar came back from a sort of sabbatical leave spent in one of the Eastern penitentiaries. It was a beautiful day; the tide on San Francisco Bay was high and the water was lapping at the San Quentin shore while the sea gulls floated lazily in the sky. The hills around the prison were green and lush with spring flowers, and down on the rocks a couple of our town youngsters were idly fishing for bass. That day, at least, San Quentin justified its reputation—the opinion of permanent guests notwithstanding—as one of the prettiest pieces of real estate in Marin County. As we walked up the long cement walk bordering the water between the gate and my office, the old man began to look around incredulously. The yellow gun towers on the hills, which once stood guard like soldiers and whose deadly marksmen had winged more than one fleeing man, were cobwebbed and empty. Along the street—our Main Street—dozens of men were working on various projects, and I spoke to some of them by name, asking about their wives and families and how the kids were getting along in school. Their work clothes were blue and neatly pressed, and the telltale shirt numbers were gone. There wasn't a guard in sight, and they were talking like workmen in any other town, in a language anyone could understand.

"They don't look like no cons to me," the old-timer said suspiciously.

"They're not," I said. "They're inmates. We don't use the word convict around here any more, and they won't let you forget it."

We walked on toward the admission gate where the old Spanish buildings, once a muddy gray, now sparkled in fresh green paint. In a large sunny room just to the right of the gate a dozen civilians were patronizing the San Quentin Hobby Counter, a retail shop as modern and well stocked with handmade goods as any similar store outside. In the visitors' room beyond we could see inmates talking, laughing, or clasping hands across the tables with their sweethearts and wives. There was a poster on the wall listing the prison's week-end movie fare, and from somewhere inside we could hear the prison orchestra rehearsing the latest bebop. For a moment the old-timer was speechless, and at last he turned to go inside with the officer who brought him.

"Movies, jazz bands, department stores!" he muttered. "No gun towers on the hills, no shirt numbers! Dammit, Warden, I ain't gonna like having to like this place. It's just a trick to make me work. I shouldn't have to come here."

I knew what the old man meant, and I suppose by comparison the new San Quentin might look like a country club to him. But he would not forget, as the public often does, that San Quentin is still a prison. Its men are prisoners, controlled, locked up, stripped of their rights as citizens, doing time to pay their debt. Confinement in itself is punishment, whether for a day or forever, but California's Department of Corrections feels that confinement need not be without hope, or the chance to remake shattered lives.

I wondered how the old man would feel after he got inside, because I knew he had much more to see. He would find the black dungeons gone, with the straps and rubber hose, and would see that none of the guards had clubs. He would hear about the movies and the quiz shows on Condemned Row and how the men there forget the shadow of death with chess tournaments, impromptu concerts, or just bull sessions in the long airy hall where they gather every day. He would find himself eating hot meals from a cafeteria tray, and there would be no gun guard restlessly pacing the catwalk over his head. He would no longer be cut off from the world in his cell, for he would find a radio headset there. or a copy of the new prison biweekly with all the big house news. He would no longer hear the metallic march of many gun guards on the cell-block rail, and he could smoke tailor-made cigarettes or cigars bought with his own earnings from the new San Quentin Canteen without getting into a jam. He would find he could leave his cell after dark and walk unescorted to night school, or to the big mess hall to watch the San Quentin All-Stars play their basketball rivals from towns around the bay. If he had been known as a drunk, the Alcoholics Anonymous group would soon sign him up, or if he were interested in the motivations of crime, he might find some answer in the Seekers' club. He might even get elected to the prison "house of representatives" and discuss important inmate problems in a big hall where no guard goes unless he is invited by the men. And he might see me walking alone through thousands of so-called "dangerous" men in the yard—men going out tomorrow, and men who will never be free, the bad men and the good men of my town. He might even tell me I'm crazy to take the risk. But I don't need any guards for that walk. I never will. San Quentin is my home, and these are my people.

THE SAN QUENTIN STORY

1 Years ago, when I was applying for my first job in San Francisco, my prospective employer asked me where I was born. "In prison," I said. I know it was an impudent answer, and it startled him so that it probably cost me the job, even though I hastily explained that my mother was not in a cell at the time. It was an answer of habit, more or less, because as youngsters we San Quentin kids felt we belonged to a very special world, "Prison Town." There weren't very many children in the world who could say they were born in the big house—and, as kids will, we made the most of it, even though others might have considered it a blot on their name. I can recall going to the women's cell block long ago, before they were transferred to a prison of their own, to cheer up some unhappy girl who had come to prison not knowing she was pregnant. "Oh, please, please, get me out of here before it's too late," she would weep. "Think of the disgrace for my baby—how would you feel if you'd been born here?" And of course I always answered, "I was born here," even though that gave small comfort. Now, starting my second

half century at San Quentin, it no longer seems important, but it still surprises people.

My father, William Joseph Duffy, owned a small farm in the then hot and dusty village of San Pablo, just across the bay from Point San Quentin. Dad didn't like farming; he used to say he preferred to stay inside the house and mind the children while Mother was in the barn milking the cows. One day the late Sheriff R. R. Veale, of Contra Costa County, an old family friend, told my father there was a vacancy at San Quentin, a guard job paying fifty dollars a month.

"Well, Sheriff," he said, "only one trouble about that. I've been a justice of the peace around here, as you know, and some of the fellows I was instrumental in sending to San Quentin are still there."

"Don't give it a worry," said Veale. "They'll respect you all the more."

Dad decided to take a chance, and told Warden W. E. Hale he could start work at once. The whole Duffy family —there were already five children—moved into a little white house at San Quentin in 1894, and I was born there four years later. Dad went on duty just about the time Warden Hale unwillingly officiated at the first execution of a white man at San Quentin. Some months before, Hale had been sheriff of Alameda County, where, like other county sheriffs, he was occasionally compelled to execute a man. Hale agitated for a new law that would relieve the sheriffs of this unpleasant duty and transfer all executions to the state prison. He sponsored the bill himself and was thankful when it was voted into law. Then, by a twist of fate, he was appointed warden at San Quentin and almost immediately was called upon to hang a man. The unfortunate gallows pioneer was a burly Irishman named P. J. Sullivan who had murdered his wife in San Francisco, and my father was as upset as though the condemned man had been a personal friend.

" 'Tis a fine welcome I'm getting," he said. "They're hiring one Irishman, then hanging another to make it even."

The old house we lived in is gone now, but whenever I pass the spot I can still see my father standing there with a rifle—one night after the 1906 San Francisco fire, when I first realized that our life was quite different from that of ordinary families. The San Francisco police had evacuated the jails, loaded the prisoners into a boat, and had anchored offshore opposite our house. There was a rumor that the prisoners were plotting to seize the boat because the authorities wanted to lock them up inside the prison until order was restored in San Francisco. There was an attorney named George D. Collins aboard the boat, a fiery man who had been in the city jail when the earthquake began. "You'll not put me or any of us in the penitentiary even for an hour!" he roared from the boat deck. "I know the law and I'll sue you to the highest court." Actually Collins had already been convicted of perjury in connection with a bigamous marriage and sentenced to San Quentin for fifteen years. But that day he was still a county jail prisoner, even though he eventually lost his case, and he had an undebatable point of law in his favor. The visiting jailbirds were allowed to stay aboard the boat. Even so, Warden John Edgar thought there might be trouble, and he had worried San Quentin guards patrol the water front. "Now look, kids," my father said. "Go on and play and forget those poor fellows on the boat. They're probably wet and hungry and scared, and they're not going to bother anybody." Nothing happened, of course, and the boat moved away in a few days. But I never forgot the incident, and ever since I've thought of men behind bars as my father saw them—human beings in trouble and needing a helping hand.

Childhood at San Quentin then was a little different than it is for the youngsters who live there today. The neat little blue suits I wore as a boy, for instance, were made from my father's worn-out guard uniforms. Like other boys, I had a paper route, but mine ran from the front gate to the warden's office, and over to the captain's desk, and I didn't dare lose a copy when prisoners were around, because the local papers were contraband. We climbed forbidden trees, usually the pomegranates around the warden's house, or those in a tiny orchard below the east gate gun tower. There was one favorite pear tree there from which we stole fruit, usually on dark nights. Charlie White and I put on fake wrestling matches on the boardwalk below the gun tower and tossed our caps around as the guard watched from above. After ten minutes or so we were throwing our caps clear out of sight under the pear tree, and in retrieving them we always managed to swipe half a dozen pears. We were never "caught," because the tower guards were tolerant, and it was a long time before it occurred to me that any prisoner who tried to steal those same pears would have been shot at, or at best sent to the dungeon for a month.

We went fishing, too, but we were never out of sight of the tower guns. Instead of cops-and-robbers we played prisoners-and-guards, but there was always an argument, because very few of the boys wanted to be guards. We knew scores of prisoners by their first names. They were our friends and "neighbors," and some of them took great risks to steal ice cream from the officers' mess and smuggle it out to us. On Sundays we would hike up the north hill, and from there we could look down into the main yard. We could see a swarming mass of men in stripes, and a few who were forced to wear red shirts so they would be a better target for the riflemen patrolling the walls. We heard shots once in a while, and at night, if we were outside, the wind would sometimes carry the screams of men laced up in their punishing jackets.

I don't think we ever realized, as children, that we were living and growing up in a constricted world where fear and cruelty were commonplace, where family laughter and horseplay served as a convenient and necessary mask for the tension under which our parents lived. Even the daily risks my father faced were not very real to me, and it was years before I understood why he came home one night with something hidden in his coat, and why he took my mother into another room and whispered a story he didn't want us to hear.

That morning, it seems, a giant murderer named Delehanty had started out grimly after two men he had sworn to kill. He had an eighteen-inch shiv, a dagger made from a file, and before guards could snatch it away he had run down his quarry, murdering one man and seriously wounding the other. Then he bounded into the big yard, scattering a dozen men working there, and bellowed that next he was going to knock off a couple of guards. My father saw him coming and went out to meet him, unarmed.

"Delehanty," he said quietly, "I am ashamed of you. Give me the shiv."

The killer stopped short and stared at my father wordlessly for a full minute. Then he loosened the straps that had bound the weapon to his wrist and handed it over. "Duffy," he said, "I wouldn't do this for any other man alive." Delehanty was subsequently hanged, and my father's reward for his courage was the privilege of being allowed to keep the shiv as a souvenir. I still have the weapon at home, a reminder that even the most savage of men need and appreciate a friend. My father, in truth, was more of a friend than jailer to hundreds of San Quentin's men. He was self-conscious about weapons, among other things, and never used the club that all guards carried at the time. Dad was a poor marksman, too, and for years he was afraid he would lose his job because he made such a miserable showing at the weekly target shoots. During those early years, after an evening in the saloon just outside the gate, Dad would come home fuming over the injustices inflicted on prisoners every day. More than once he threatened to resign, but Mother knew it was just a bluff and that he would never fail those unhappy men behind walls, men who needed a gentle and understanding heart. I can still remember a little verse the prisoners used to chant, a poem called *Duffy's on the Wall,* and when the Duffy family gets together we sing it to remind ourselves of the long ago. It goes like this:

The guards stood in their boxes,
The bell tolled six o'clock;
A band of faithful trustees
Were grinding out the locks.
The signal soon was given,
All answered to the call;
Then Al'a'men left,
For Duffy's on the wall.

Translated, the verse simply meant that when the cells were opened for the nightly lockup, all the prisoners fell in line and everything was under control as long as Duffy was at his post on the wall.

During those early years, if any of our bunch wanted a straight answer to a question about the prison, we could usually get it from Johnny Carpenter, a stocky, walrus-mustached guard who was my father's friend and neighbor and who later became Captain of the Yard. Awed prisoners used to say that Captain Carpenter could outroar the foghorns on the bay, but his twinkling blue eyes usually gave him away. Of all the thousands he judged behind walls—quickly and with uncanny perception—not one ever complained that Captain Johnny gave him a raw deal. Principals in a disciplinary case could read his decisions before he spoke—he invariably twisted his mustache if he believed the prisoner was wrong, or jammed his big hands into his hip pockets if he thought the guard had erred. The legends say that Mrs. Carpenter was always repairing the pockets on his official pants, but that the ends of his mustache never did get curled. "Son," he said to me one day, "if you're going to stick around here, remember this:

21

there's no such thing as a criminal class. Sometimes the difference between a good man and a bad man is just about the distance between the cell blocks and the first foot of free ground outside."

As the years went on I spent more and more time at the Carpenter house, especially in the evenings. My father thought I was showing an encouraging interest in penology, but actually I was studying the problem of solitary confinement with the captain's pretty blond daughter, Gladys. One summer day, long after we were graduated from San Rafael High School, Gladys and I went to a Shrine picnic. The gate prize was a gold wedding ring—and I won it. The ring was a perfect fit—and still is—but I've often wondered if the raffle wasn't fixed.

San Quentin's boys and girls rarely come back after they've gone to school. They move to other towns and they stay away. They shut out from their nostalgia the endless turning of locks, the bonging of the big bell that ends the day's cell count, the morning siren, the copper spire that carries off the deadly fumes from the gas chamber, the never-ending inspection of cars that pass through the gates, the march of lonely women going up our main street to see their imprisoned men. Gladys and I went away, too, after our marriage on December 31, 1921, but, unlike most others, our hearts were still in San Quentin. After my discharge from the United States Marine Corps at the end of World War I, I worked for a railroad in Marin County for a while, but I could still see the high walls and hear the sounds. I took a job with a construction company a quarter of a mile from San Quentin's hills, and I could hear the lockup bells and the runners calling men to the visiting room. One day in 1929 I went to San Quentin to notarize a document—fortunately I had just been made a notary—and overheard Warden Holohan telling his secretary, Rivera Smith, that they needed another office assistant.

"Pardon me for butting in, Warden," I said. "How about giving me that job?"

He thought it over for a moment, then looked at me speculatively. "All right. If you want it, you've got it."

I was home again, at last.

James B. Holohan, a hulking, curly-haired, and rather handsome man, had come to San Quentin two years previously with a reputation as a poker-faced, two-gun peace officer of "the old West." He had once been a sheriff, but his quick-trigger fame was the result of a spectacular affair in San Francisco during the first World War while he was United States Marshal. One Hindu defendant in an espionage case killed another in a crowded federal courtroom, whereupon Holohan whipped out a gun and drilled the assassin with a single shot. "You know, Clinton," he confided one day, "every time I see the men inside I think they expect me to pull a six-shooter. The fact is that I never shot a man in my life until that day in court, and haven't pointed a gun at anyone since. I just took a chance, and I would probably do it again."

I liked and admired Warden Holohan, even though we disagreed in principle much of the time, and I was grateful for his confidence in me. During the seven years I sat at the front desk outside his office he sent me everywhere in the prison on special assignments. I had to soothe weeping mothers whose son were doing their first term and calm screaming gang molls who insisted that cruel guards were slowly killing their guys.

I learned something about real courage, too, from hundreds of wives and mothers, those unsung "prisoners" outside the walls who often suffer more than the men inside. Whenever I hear a man growling about doing time I remember a quiet little woman with five children—let's call her Mrs. Howard—who was left destitute in Los Angeles when her husband was imprisoned. Broke and friendless, she recalled that the family owned a small piece of good land in the resort section of Clear Lake, in northern California. The property was six hundred miles north of Los Angeles, but she determined to get there and sell it, first pausing at San Quentin to get a signed release from her husband. She piled the five kids into a wheezy old Ford and started out. Toward the end of that first day the ancient car burned out a connecting rod, and to her dismay the mother was forced to use all her cash for repairs. Most women would have quit and gone to a state agency for relief. But Mrs. Howard herded her children into a cheap auto court, unearthed a small sack of sugar from a battered suitcase, and cooked up a batch of fudge. She sent the kids out to sell the candy from door to door, and used the proceeds to buy more sugar for more fudge. In two days she earned enough to pay for the cabin and gasoline for the rest of the trip. When the family arrived at San Quentin the creaking car was spouting like a geyser, and the mother had a single dollar in her purse. I took up a collection for her around the office, and Warden Holohan, who knew a gallant lady when he saw one, sent the Ford to the prison garage, where enthusiastic inmate mechanics soon had it purring like a custom job. The "Fudge Lady," as she came to be known, rode on to Clear Lake a few days later, sold the property, then started for home. On the outskirts of Los Angeles the ill-fated car burst into flames, and Mrs. Howard scorched her hands rescuing the children. But a few days later she had found a clean little shack and was dipping her burned fingers into hot water, doing other people's laundry so she wouldn't have to use her small capital. She wrote us a poignant note of thanks and asked us to tell her husband she was doing fine. I've often wondered where she is. I would like to tell the "Fudge Lady" that the "thank you" note should have been written by us— because she taught us something unforgettable about a valiant heart.

My training period also involved me in the investigation of suicides, hunger strikes, mental breakdowns, and cases in which some trigger-happy guards wounded or occasionally killed prisoners who ran amuck in the yard. I spent a lot of time, too, on what we used to call the "prima donna" circuit, a routine that involved occasional checkups on prisoners who made news almost every time they sneezed.

The patriarch of this difficult clan, of course, was Tom Mooney, the so-called labor martyr who spent most of his prison years personally guiding the world-wide campaign for his release. Mooney was an Olympian figure behind walls, imperious and arrogant in his reiterated innocence and in his pretense that he was not in a prison at all, but in a self-chosen place of exile. He irritated other prisoners by his unique position, and his outgoing mail was often so vitriolic that when I was asked to censor it I simply wrote across it one word: "No." He took these rejections as a personal affront, and would scold me in what was certainly indelicate language, but on the whole he was a co-operative inmate. The question of Mooney's guilt or innocence in the San Francisco parade bomb case was not our problem, of course, but privately we felt that he wouldn't be able to maintain his position outside. He was eventually pardoned by Governor Olson and, as we predicted, soon became the forgotten man. He was a lonely and disillusioned man when he died in Santa Barbara not long after his release.

Two other "celebrities" of the period were Kid Mc-Coy, the amorous prize fighter who accidentally killed his sweetheart, Theresa Moers, during a colossal drinking spree, and Bluebeard Watson, the mousy little man who, it is said, murdered twenty wives by twisting their necks and dropping their weighted bodies into deep water.

The Kid was a cheerful prisoner who used to warm himself in the sun outside the San Quentin firehouse and reminisce about the days when he was "the real McCoy." I always thought of him as a child at heart, racing to catch up with a world that had somehow outgrown his antics in the ring, or in boudoirs from coast to coast. Kid McCoy spent seven years in San Quentin, an amiable and garrulous man who never broke a prison rule. The Kid wore an aura of sad splendor, the lambent light of the past when he was the cocky darling of the ring. The shimmer was in his Gaelic banter, and the crinkle of his eyes, and the dainty shadowboxing he used to do outside my office when he felt especially gay. He lamented only that he was never allowed to do any ring fighting in prison or teach his immortal corkscrew punch to the lads who hoped for a prize-fight career when they had done their time. Once Warden Holohan relented, when the Kid was working at a prison road camp, and sent him a pair of boxing gloves and a punching bag. The Kid had rescued a plane pilot who crashed in the rocky hills of the San Simeon road along the Pacific coast, and Warden Holohan thought he had earned that small reward. "Thanks for the gloves and the bag, Warden," he wrote back. "They'll keep me in shape until I can get back to the firehouse. If you have any secondhand paroles around, I could use those too." Kid McCoy's wise-cracks, which were snapped up by every newspaperman who came to see him at San Quentin, kept him in the public prints throughout the years, and I suspect that he lay awake at night, grinning and coining new ones he could toss casually at the next visitor. *Woman was made from a rib,* he would chuckle, *and she's still a ticklish problem.* Or, if he were in a philosophical mood, he would shake a pudgy finger and say: *Remember that the bright lights go out the quickest. Kid McCoy knows.* Someone has since suggested that Kid McCoy's epigrams were not entirely original and that he may have unwittingly been plagiarizing another famed San Quentin inmate named William Hightower. For the past thirty years Hightower, who was convicted of kidnaping and murdering a Catholic priest in a now classic case, has been manufacturing quips for the amusement of the inmate body. He has put them down on paper, a sort of one-man syndicate, and passed them around for his friends to read. The Hightower wisecracks are strikingly similar to Kid McCoy's pearls of humor, or vice versa, but the question may never be settled.

But the Kid was proud of one thing that no one will quarrel about—the fact that he contributed an imperishable phrase to the language—"the real McCoy." "I'm not sure how it started," he explained to me one day, "except that I was in a saloon with a charming young lady, as usual, and a drunk was making big eyes at her. I tried to brush him off quiet-like. 'I'm Kid McCoy,' I told him. 'Beat it.' So he laughs at me and says: 'Yeah? Well, I'm Julius Caesar.' I have to clip him a short one. Ten minutes later he wakes up rubbing his chin and says: 'Jesus! It *was* the real McCoy!'"

Someone was always sending a gift to the Kid—a box of figs, a jar of jam, mayonnaise, or persimmons, and he always shared them with his mates in the firehouse where he worked. Lionel Barrymore, who knew the Kid in his youth, sent him cash, and Sophie Tucker traded quips with him in the visitors' room. There was many a man around San Quentin who wondered why the Kid had it so good, but none of them knew that the jurors and the district attorney who sent him to prison had openly voiced their doubts about his guilt. Subsequently, when the Kid asked for parole, he was backed by the most remarkable list of sponsors ever offered to a parole board in San Quentin. The signers included Vice President Curtis, General Douglas MacArthur, Alfred E. Smith, six United States senators, six state governors, and scores of congressmen, mayors, financiers, movie stars, and sportsmen. The Kid won his freedom, and we saw him off one day in 1932, a balding, broken old man carrying a canary in a little wooden cage and anticipating his tenth and last marriage. I got a postcard or two from him later that year, with brave little gags about his new job at the Ford Motor Company, but his heart was already dead, and he killed himself with sleeping pills in Detroit not long afterward. "It's no fun telling people you're Kid McCoy," he used to say, "if they've never heard of you before."

James P. ("Bluebeard") Watson, who for years was confined in the prison hospital with tuberculosis, was a querulous, fussy little man constantly embroiled in quarrels with newspapermen, lawyers, and other people outside the walls. Warden Holohan, who was weary of Bluebeard's eternal carping, turned him over to me and I came to know him quite well. Bluebeard was strangely proud of the fact that he, probably one of the world's ugliest creatures, had literally charmed a score of women to death, and he urged me to remember that "soft words make for a soft touch."

During his twenty years in San Quentin, Bluebeard puzzled and exasperated four wardens. He was a sort of penological museum piece, classified as a homicidal monster, yet curiously gentle and shy, and he fascinated the public. Warden Jim Johnston once said dourly: "I had to turn away a number of women who had no legitimate reason for calling but who faked excuses in the hope of getting a chance to see him." On the other hand, I was never surprised at the continuing public interest in Bluebeard because, among other things, he was probably the only mass murderer of modern times who was not executed for his crimes. It so happened that none of his victims ever showed up, dead or alive, to furnish any sort of *corpus delicti*. The police might still be working on the case if Bluebeard, shrewdly bargaining with the district attorney in Los Angeles, had not offered to produce one (1) corpse in exchange for life imprisonment. He showed the authorities where he had buried Miss Nina Lee Deloney in the desert south of Los Angeles, after chopping her with an ax, and was duly given the life sentence he wanted. As one consequence of this deal, Bluebeard was besieged in prison with letters, telegrams, and personal visits from bereaved men and women who wanted to know where he had buried their loved ones. Bluebeard toyed with these people in an almost fiendish sort of game, coyly hinting, but never revealing, and to this day no one knows exactly how many women he slew or where he hid their bodies. Despite his fearful record, this five-foot-five man with the square face, underslung jaw, and wispy hair continued to attract women, and I have no doubt he could have had another dozen eager wives if he had been set free.

Cannily, Bluebeard never asked for parole, suspecting that other states would put him on trial without the same consideration he got in Los Angeles. But he was acutely aware of his infamy, and carried on a lively correspondence with autograph collectors, writers, editors, anthropologists, criminologists, and others who were interested in his bloody career. He willingly furnished exemplars of his handwriting, his fingerprints, and Bertillon measurements to those who requested them, and finally he decided to write for publication. "Though legally dead," he said to me, "I can think, pen my thoughts, and sell them." I was able to obtain a typewriter for him to keep him busy—he was unable to do much work—and for years afterward he poured out a stream of poems, essays, short stories, and confessions which, he complained, the nation's editors never appreciated. He invariably typed his name on these manuscripts as "Bluebeard Watson," but objected bitterly when my friend, author Jim Tully, wrote about him and used the same phrase. I saw Bluebeard quite often during the last ten years of his life, when he was a devoted orderly to Dr. Leo Stanley, San Quentin's chief physician, and helped him arrange his affairs when he knew he had not long to live. He confided that he had an enormous fortune in a secret hiding place and promised we would all have a ·part of it. Dr. Stanley and I always nodded gravely when Bluebeard discussed his wealth, and we humored him when he insisted on making his will. When he died in 1939, I was surprised to find myself designated as executor of his estate. The will, which was a remarkable document in many ways, disposed of some eighty thousand dollars in cash and jewels—the proceeds, presumably, of his homicides. I was bequeathed one third of his fortune, with the rest going to Warden Holohan, Dr. Stanley, Guard Lieutenant Dan Coughlin, the Salvation Army, the Volunteers of America, and—for some unexplained reason—Henry L. Mencken. "The location of the money," Watson wrote in his will, "will be revealed in another document." I never found this other document, or any further clues. I don't think there ever was any hidden wealth. But even today— eleven years after his death—I still get an occasional letter from indignant families in other states, including relatives of Bluebeard's victims, demanding their share of my spoils. I always tell them what he really had—a trunk full of florid prose and a prison bank account with $18.70. I like to think of Watson, in the twilight of his life, secretly enjoying the gossip about his wealth and giggling to himself as he wrote his will. There, at least, was a document from his typewriter that no one would ignore.

Condemned Row also had its share of temperament

and bad actors. The first time Warden Holohan sent me to the Row—which was then on the second tier of the old Spanish cell block—I was confronted with a suicide which baffled our doctors. The victim in this rare occurrence was a young bank robber named Red O'Brien who had sworn— like scores of doomed men before him—that he would cheat the state. He got away with it all right, using a fast-acting poison. It was weeks before we discovered that his girl, kissing him good-by just a few days before the scheduled execution, had passed him a poison capsule with her lips. Ever since, condemned men with last-minute visitors are carefully searched before they go back to their cells.

Warden Holohan favored capital punishment, because he felt that if men were imprisoned without hope of parole as a substitute for the death penalty, they would be "the most desperate, fiendish men on the face of the earth" and would stop at nothing—including more murders—to get out. Nevertheless, he suffered intensely when he had to officiate at executions, and often asked me to go along for moral support. Whenever possible, I backed out, inventing excuses of one kind or another. Long before I returned to San Quentin I had determined never to witness an execution, and at least once had refused an invitation from my father-in-law, Captain Carpenter. He had asked me to attend the hanging of the notorious William Edward Hickman, the so-called "Fox" who kidnaped and dismembered a little girl named Marian Parker. More than one thousand persons had begged for "tickets" to the execution, people lashed to a morbid frenzy by gory newspaper accounts of this twenty-year-old boy's confession, and Captain Carpenter thought I might have some professional curiosity about the case. I was spending much of my spare time at San Quentin and was interested in everything that happened there, of course, but, like my father, I balked at going to hangings. I kept this resolve until October 2, 1930, when Warden Holohan more or less ordered me to assist at the execution of a repulsive young homosexual named Gordon Stewart Northcott. At nine o'clock that morning the baby-faced murderer had been found writhing on the floor of the death cell, screaming that he had swallowed poison. Dr. Stanley went to work on him with a stomach pump, but when we reached the cell Northcott was still trembling and sobbing that the rope was going to hurt.

"I never have heard anyone complain about its hurting," Dr. Stanley said quietly.

"I want a blindfold over my eyes . . ." Northcott cried. "Let me walk slowly . . ."

Warden Holohan, pale and plainly suffering, nodded to the guards. They quickly tied a black bandage around the boy's eyes and the death march began. I hung back as we entered the high gallows room on the top floor of the crumbling furniture factory, and Warden Holohan turned his eyes away from the rope. Northcott stumbled and sagged, and the guards carried him up the steps. I heard him weeping and he said: "Say a prayer for me . . . please." Warden Holohan raised his right hand, a tired and unwilling hand, and it was over. That night, sitting alone with Gladys, I said: "I'm glad I'm not the warden. I'll never do that again." But I was wrong.

On another Friday morning, shortly before ten o'clock, Warden Holohan had gone alone to the gallows room to officiate at a hanging. I stayed behind deliberately because

I knew the condemned man and had grown fond of him during the long months he fought his case. I was sitting at the warden's desk, self-consciously watching the minute hand on the electric wall clock, when the phone rang. I picked it up and identified myself.

"Hello, Duffy," a voice shrilled. "This is the governor's secretary in Sacramento. You have an execution this morning."

"Yes. The warden's up there now."

"Well, stop it! Get on the phone. The governor has some new evidence and has signed a reprieve."

I asked him to wait, and I snatched up another phone. I got a fast connection to the death cells adjoining the gallows room, and one of the guards answered.

"Have they started yet?" I asked.

"Yes, sir. They just went in——" There was a breathless pause, and I heard a crashing sound. "There goes the trap now. Did you hear it? Are you there, Mr. Duffy?"

I hung up, and listlessly picked up the other phone. "You're too late," I said. "The man's been hanged."

I could hear him suck in his breath. "Duffy . . ." he said very slowly, "forget what I just said. Forget I ever called. If you ever say anything about this, the governor and I will both deny it. Don't even tell the warden. Understand?"

"I understand."

Warden Holohan never knew about this incident, nor did anyone else. The governor and his secretary are both dead, and so, alas, is the man who might not have been hanged. To me this case alone is a compelling argument against capital punishment, without considering any other factors involved. It so happens that the victim of this error —whose name I can't reveal for obvious reasons—had confessed his crime and knew that only a technicality could save him. I have never known what new evidence the governor had, and perhaps it would have made no difference. But a man at the end of a rope is very, very dead and in no position to argue the merits of his case.

Not long after this miserable affair, which kept gnawing at my mind, there was another execution which Warden Holohan and I both attended. We had called the governor's office and were told to proceed. The prisoner was hustled up the thirteen wooden steps, planted on the white-painted trap, and swiftly noosed. Warden Holohan nodded and the hangman's right arm flew up as a signal to three guards who were hidden in the trap control booth. They slashed at the trap cords with sharp knives, but nothing happened. Warden Holohan gave the executioner a wild and imploring look, and the prisoner began to sway. It was the first time in prison history that the trap failed to work, and I made a dive for the heavy ropes leading down from the control booth. A guard got there first, yanked the rope, and the trap fell.

An hour later, still shaky, Warden Holohan and I were discussing the curious failure of the trap when he got a long-distance call from the condemned man's lawyer.

"You know what you've done!" he yelled. "You've hanged a man illegally. I filed an appeal on that case and the court was still considering it."

"That's news to me," said Holohan.

"Oh, no it isn't. I sent you a registered letter telling you about the appeal."

The warden was dumfounded. He hadn't seen the letter, and I couldn't recall it either. Later that day the letter turned up in a mail basket. It had been rubber-stamped "Received—Warden's Office," and on one corner were my initials. I was appalled. I now recalled putting the letter on the warden's desk with a pile of mail, but obviously he had never seen it. I don't know how the letter was mislaid, nor does anyone else. After all these years I still have an eerie feeling about this case, and if I were highly superstitious I would probably feel that some mysterious force made the trap stick that day. In any case, there were immediate repercussions. Up to that time the courts were setting execution dates when a man was convicted, and it was the responsibility of defense attorneys to file an appeal. If there was no appeal, prison wardens automatically proceeded with the hanging. The state legislature threw out this ancient system and wrote a new law providing an automatic appeal for all condemned men, stipulating that no execution date could be set until the higher court had ruled on the appeal.

At San Quentin the investigation of this fiasco was rough on all concerned, and I was all set to pack up and leave. One day I picked up the private line in the warden's office to make a call and overheard one of the state prison directors excoriating Mark Noon, the board's husky, red-haired secretary. "One more thing," the voice said, "fire Duffy immediately." But I wasn't fired. Mark Noon fought for me, insisting that it wasn't my fault. Some years later, when a new warden came in, Noon took me in as his assistant, a gesture of friendship and confidence that eventually changed the whole course of my life.

2 I don't suppose I will ever forget Albert M. Stewart, even though his name or his crime would mean very little to anyone in San Quentin today.

Stewart was not a criminal mastermind, or a spectacular murderer, or even a good burglar. He was known only as "The Squealer," a gaunt, sunken-eyed man shunned by other inmates because, long years before, he had given testimony that sent five of his fellow prisoners to the gallows after a bloody riot at·Folsom, the rocky prison fortress more or less reserved for California's habitual criminals. I used to see him shuffling around our big yard alone, afraid of the gun towers, afraid of other men, and afraid of himself. Yet Albert Stewart, the outcast, unwittingly set off a chain reaction of trouble that made my apprenticeship under Warden Holohan seem like one disaster after another.

One quiet afternoon in the fall of 1933, Stewart suddenly appeared at the threshold of the distribution office inside the walls. He was wearing a belt studded with ominous-looking brown sticks which were connected by bell wire to a large dry battery in his right hand. "This is dynamite," he said very quietly to Officer Walter Gillette. "Get me a truck. We're goin' out." Gillette was wondering whether he could bluff it out when another prisoner jumped Stewart from behind and yanked the battery out of his hand. By the time I reached the office the little drama was over and Stewart was slumped in a chair, weeping in his loneliness and frustration. Even his "dynamite" sticks were no good, for they were only pieces of broom handle, wrapped in brown paper and painted to look like the real thing. We transferred Stewart to Folsom—he has since been released and is now serving a new term in a Canadian prison—and wrote off the incident as another case of a man gone stir-crazy.

But things began to happen. Little things at first. A squabble in the mess line, a fist fight in the yard. Then, a week or so later, a man threw a lighted match into one of the jute-mill looms with its oily hemp, and there was a near riot before the fire was controlled. Still later a gun guard shot a man in the yard, and we heard rumors of an impending break. There was no obvious link between any of these incidents. But there was a connection nevertheless—the tenuous thread of unrest, the contagion of misery. San Quentin was jammed; more than six thousand men were living—if you could call it living—in cells and basement dormitories meant for half that many. Attorney General Homer Cummings, who visited San Quentin at that time, went back to Washington saying: "It was the most depressing experience of my life." We felt the tension in the warden's office, too, and our nerves were frazzled, with the result that sometimes we, and the prisoners, too, lost patience over trivial things.

One day, for example, a young fellow was brought in to discuss a government disability pension form. He had been in the army, and I explained that he would start getting pension payments as soon as he signed the papers.

"I won't sign," he said. "I never liked the army and I don't want any of their dough."

"Oh, all right," I said irritably. "Go back to your cell."

I turned my back on him, and presently, after standing there silently for a moment, he went out. I reported my failure to Captain Breakfield, who suggested mildly that I probably didn't understand this prisoner and offered to handle the case himself. He sent for the sullen young man, tried the same arguments I had used, and finally gave up, ordering the prisoner to leave. But this time the man didn't go. He whipped out a knife and stabbed Captain Breakfield seven times before other guards arrived and knocked him out. Captain Breakfield nearly died. It could have happened to me, and for a while I wondered why I had given up a comfortable job outside to come "home" to San Quentin. I have since become very fatalistic about my work, but now I don't deliberately turn my back on an argumentative man.

During this period of uneasiness, when Warden Holohan was struggling with an inadequate budget and a few incompetent guards, there were reporters in the office nosing around for news almost every day, and their presence began to irritate the warden. Sometimes he flatly refused to see them, and if they had any specific requests, he was apt to growl at me: "Tell 'em to go to hell. Get 'em off the lot." When he was in such a mood I simply closed the office door quietly, went outside to the waiting reporters, and said: "The warden says he'll be happy to co-operate, fellows. Now, what can we do for you?"

I have always thought the newspapers knew that the situation at San Quentin early in 1934 was almost untenable and were just waiting for the inevitable backfire. These were the dark days of the depression; there were few jobs for parolees, juries were getting tougher, and hundreds of new prisoners were pouring through the gates every month. At one time we had seven Los Angeles millionaires doing time for embezzlement, stock juggling, grand theft, and similar crimes, and I was kept busy denying the most absurd stories that these men were being pampered and allowed to spend week ends in San Francisco hotels. One indignant editor insisted that one of these financial barons was driving the warden's car to San Francisco, and was not convinced until I took him to the big mess hall and pointed out the man busily mopping the tile floor. Condemned Row was also crowded. In just a few months Warden Holohan had wearily climbed the steep iron stairs to the gallows room seven times, and he would go there seven times more before the year was out. There were at least a dozen men capable of starting something that might turn into a major riot or break, and we didn't have enough guards to watch them all day and night.

One morning in March, I left my house about eight o'clock and started for the office, which was only a few hundred feet up the street. It was wet and chilly, and the fog swirling in from the bay was so thick that I almost missed the turnoff to the Administration Building. I was just going in the door when I heard a shot, then two more in rapid succession. I crossed the street and started running. I bumped into several people I couldn't recognize in the fog, and eventually reached Captain Breakfield's office inside the walls. All the lights were on and a guard was sprawled face down on the floor. His uniform was ripped and splashed with blood and he was groaning.

"Who is he?" I asked.

Breakfield said nothing, but reached down and flipped the man over on his back. I looked down at the thin white face and recognized him as inmate Ethan McNabb, a bank robber with a brilliant mind and a cold heart.

"He's been worked over somewhat," Breakfield said, "and if it hadn't been so damn foggy, he'd have got a slug in the head."

"Anyone else hurt?"

"Oh, sure. A prisoner named Arbuckle is dead and two or three of McNabb's pals are banged up. Couple of guards in the hospital, too."

Breakfield angrily stripped the guard uniform from McNabb, and he was carried naked to the prison hospital, where Bill Bagley, another gunman involved in the case, was already on the operating table. By the time Warden Holohan reached the scene it was already painfully obvious to us that someone had been careless in watching a known troublemaker. McNabb, who was called the "yacht bandit" because he and his partner Lloyd Sampsel escaped to sea in a luxurious cruiser each time they pulled a bank stick-up, had come to San Quentin as a transfer. He had been whisked out of Folsom Prison because he and Sampsel, a dangerous combination even behind bars, had already been involved in two escape plots and it was only a question of time before they might kill someone there.

Unfortunately, McNabb was even more noxious alone. I had seen him in the yard or at the prison library once in a while, a tense, foxy young man incongruously poring over books on machine tooling and metalcraft. None of us, I'm sure, appreciated his mechanical genius or guessed what he was trying to do. Not long after his arrival at San Quentin, McNabb acquired two or three dozen used pistol shells which had been dug up from the guards' rifle range. With amazing patience and ingenuity, McNabb hand-tooled three guns in the machine shop and loaded the empty cartridges with stolen lead and chemicals smuggled from the prison hospital. On this March morning, accompanied by Bagley and two other prisoners, McNabb marched into the prison electrical shop. Six inmate electricians, already at work, were rounded up, and McNabb began binding them with wire. Looking out the window, McNabb saw Guard Fred Miller approaching the building. He nudged one of his companions and said: "Get Miller in here. Tell him we're drinking whisky or something." The man obeyed, and Miller soon came inside to investigate. Bagley clubbed him down, and McNabb stripped off his uniform.

"Quite a stunt you fellows are pulling," Miller grunted.

"It sure is," said McNabb, " if we get away with it."

McNabb was tense and excited, and in the hasty trussing of the prisoners he got careless with his gun. The weapon went off, barely missing Miller, and a slug struck John Arbuckle, a harmless little man who had just started a term for bigamy. Arbuckle fell on his face, dead, and Bagley blurted: "My God, Mac, why did you do that?"

McNabb had a surprised look on his face. "Damn—of all the rotten luck!" he said. "That would have to happen."

But he paid no more attention to Arbuckle and went on with his work. He reloaded his gun, took a last look around, and started for the door with Bagley. "Here goes," he said. "If I get shot, I get shot. If not—okay." Seconds later, carrying a ladder and a coil of wire, McNabb yelled at Guard Ernie Williamson, who was patrolling the high wall at the No. 6 gun post. "Hey, Ernie," he said, "here's some guys to fix the power line. Give 'em a hand with the ladder." At that moment the fog lifted and Williamson got a good look at McNabb's pinched face and the ill-fitting uniform. McNabb told me later he had an uncanny feeling that the fog would disappear at that crucial moment, and he didn't wait for Williamson to ask questions. He started shooting with his queer guns. In the savage fight that followed, the pudgy Bagley was subdued with a strangle hold by Guard Fred Hogeboom, and McNabb was knocked cold with a pick handle swung by a retiring guard known as "Old Petie." The other two retreated hastily, and the battle was over in about two minutes.

Warden Holohan had always been a firm believer in the "con boss" system, because he thought seasoned prisoners could handle the men as well as some civilian guards on the work projects. He also had trusted informants in the shops and cell blocks, although he usually bristled if anyone called them stool pigeons. Nevertheless, he had not heard a whisper about McNabb's plot, and none of us ever learned exactly how he obtained the materials for his remarkable weapons. Perhaps he bought secrecy with money, for at that time a prisoner with cash could get almost any forbidden article, including whisky, drugs, cigars, and candy. Bagley actually obtained hacksaws and rope three days before his execution and got out of his cell long enough to bash in a guard's skull. McNabb wasn't cut in on this deal, but he made frantic attempts to buy some potassium cyanide with which to beat the rope. But he had only fifty dollars left, and the then prison racketeers, who had planned to get the poison from the photographic shop, told him it wasn't enough. McNabb took this setback philosophically and spent his last night on earth intently reading a textbook on steam fitting. He scolded Bagley for trembling as they stood on the gallows trap, and left us a note asking to be buried at sea, with a sarcastic postscript: "I am sure this will be pleasing to the good citizens of California, who have striven so assiduously to terminate my sojourn among them." Even in death McNabb's last wish was not granted; his relatives claimed the body and gave him a prosaic burial in a San Francisco cemetery.

I considered the case closed for almost fifteen years, but the other day the last chapter began to be written. I had gone up to Condemned Row to see a new arrival, a thin, gray-haired man whose rimless glasses, intense blue eyes, and quiet manner made him look like a scholar. But he wasn't a scholar—unless bank robbery is considered a science. His name is Lloyd Sampsel, McNabb's old partner in crime and the man who had purchased and operated the lavish yacht they used as a getaway craft years before. For two decades he had been in and out of prison, and now, convicted of killing a cashier during a San Diego robbery, he too was at the end of the road.

As a rule I do not have much trouble understanding

men and their motives, but there are things about Samp-sel's mental processes and behavior that I cannot compre-hend. As a boy he had every advantage, or perhaps it was a disadvantage, that indulgent parents can give. He was well educated, had an executive job in the restaurant chain owned by his father, and could have had a useful and suc-cessful business career. But he was constantly in trouble, and progressed from bigamy and forgery to bank robbery. Sampsel and McNabb were efficient and ruthless, with a fondness for sawed-off shotguns, machine guns, and auto-matic pistols, and carried them on their jobs. They took some twenty-five thousand dollars in their last two rob-beries together, and were finally trapped in a San Fran-cisco apartment after months of patient work by detec-tives.

At Folsom, Sampsel and McNabb once hid them-selves for six days in a tunnel cleverly carved out of the dirt beneath the prison blacksmith shop. Another time they smuggled three guns into the prison in a keg of nails, but the weapons were found before they could use them. McNabb was transferred to San Quentin, and Sampsel soon acquired a new escape-minded partner named Marty Coulson. Some years before, Coulson nearly drowned while attempting to escape in a homemade diving suit across the rough American River which flows past Folsom, and at the time he predicted he would break loose again someday. In February 1933, Sampsel and Coulson made a couple of very rudimental guns and attempted to lure Warden Smith to his office so they could kidnap him. Smith stalled while the prisoners menaced six employees in the office, and turned on the escape siren. The metallic screaming unnerved Coulson, and he killed himself with one shot through the head. Sampsel was evidently unwilling to go on alone and soon surrendered. As the years passed, Sampsel quieted down, and in 1947 he was granted a parole. He was then forty-seven years old, and presumably reformed. But in March 1948, Sampsel held up a finance-company office in San Diego, scuffled with two of the office employees, and while trying to break loose shot and killed the cashier, Arthur S. Smith.

At his trial Sampsel dumfounded the prosecutor and his own attorney with an extraordinary monologue in which he recounted all the sordid facets of his life, his various prison terms, and all his crimes. It was a suicidal oration, and the jury had no choice. "It appears to the court," the trial judge said, "that the defendant, in testifying on his own behalf, was somewhat of an egotist, and in his desire to tell of his past exploits testified to things that would not have been shown against him." He was convicted and sentenced to death—a penalty he must have wanted for himself—and he is on the Row now, waiting.

The McNabb episode should have warned us that the prison blood pressure was rising. But Warden Holohan felt he could ride out the crisis and was unwilling to make any drastic changes in the old system. In April, about a month after the McNabb fiasco, two prisoners named Wyeth and Stewart beat up a guard while they were out on a surveying job and escaped to the nearby highway. There they kidnaped two San Rafael police officers and drove all night to San Bernardino County in southern California. The next day, trapped in a road block, Wyeth and Stewart were shot to death in a duel with a sheriff's posse. Warden

Holohan brooded over this incident for weeks, and there were days when he hardly said a word to anyone in the office. I think he must have had a premonition that the worst was yet to come.

Toward the end of 1934 things were not much better at the prison, and Warden Holohan seemed unusually tired and depressed. One morning, after a particularly gruesome hanging in which the victim took a long time to die, he came back to the office sick with loathing. "I don't see how I can go through another one of these things, Clinton," he said. "If we're going to kill men—and God knows a lot of them deserve it—there must be some better way." He wouldn't drop the subject, and finally arranged to witness a lethal-gas execution at the Nevada State Penitentiary in Carson City. He came back with the conviction that the gas chamber was the most humane and painless capital punishment of all. He began badgering his friends in the state legislature about it and was making encouraging progress about the time the parole board came to San Quentin for its midmonthly meeting.

That day—it was January 16, 1935—Warden Holohan was alone in his big office when I took in the morning mail. He looked as nervous as a cat, drumming on the desk with his long fingers and rocking in his leather chair.

"Anything wrong, Warden?" I asked.

"Not a thing," he said brusquely.

He picked up a pencil and scribbled down the names of four prisoners whose file cards he wanted, presumably for the parole hearings. I took the list, and later, when I brought in the cards, he was still jittery and kept glancing at the clock.

"Something's bothering you, Warden," I said. "What can I do to help?"

He began shuffling the file cards, like a poker player waiting for someone to open the pot. "It's nothing, Clinton," he said at last. "Nothing at all." I knew he was holding out on me, but I had long since learned not to press him. At noon he stepped into his big black sedan and was driven to the warden's mansion on the hill to have lunch with the members of the parole board. About half an hour later, as I left the office, a popeyed inmate rushed up to me and blurted, "There's trouble at the warden's house. You better hurry." Instead of going the long way by car, I bounded up three flights of cement steps to the upper road. I could see the gun guard in No. 19 tower covering the road with his automatic rifle, and at that instant Warden Holohan's official car whizzed around the curve and almost knocked me down. I couldn't see who was in it, but the rocketing car must have had a pass, because the tower guard didn't shoot. I ran the next fifty yards to the house, arriving there almost simultaneously with Dr. Leo Stanley, the prison medical officer. We found Warden Holohan lying on the floor in a puddle of blood with his frightened wife cradling his head, and at that moment I wouldn't have given five cents for his chances. He had been savagely beaten and soon lost consciousness.

It didn't take long to find out what had happened. Four prisoners, all of whom had records as killers and kidnapers, had invaded the dining room while Warden Holohan was lunching with Frank Sykes, Warren Atherton, and Joseph Stephens, the parole board members, and Mark Noon, board secretary. The prisoners had four .45

automatics and they were in no mood to argue. They ordered the five officials to take off their clothes and threatened to kill the first man who refused. Warden Holohan, who had been staring at the guns openmouthed, suddenly rebelled at this affront to his dignity and position. He turned his back on Rudolph Straight, the leader of the gang, walked into the next room, and calmly reached for the telephone. Straight was after him in a flash. He fired a shot that thudded into the wall—the bullet is still there today—and then smashed Warden Holohan to the floor with the butt of his gun. Straight would have killed the warden if Fred Landers, one of the conspirators, had not interfered and told him to "lay off." Straight, satisfied that Holohan couldn't call for help, went back into the dining room and began barking orders. Minutes later, wearing the civilian clothes they had taken from their victims, the four inmates herded the parole board men and two guards into the warden's car and roared down the hill. We learned that the speeding car had just gone out through the west gate, which had been left open by Mark Noon's order. The car raced through the town of San Rafael and took the main highway north. Guard Lieutenant Harry Jones, who had been forced into the machine at the warden's house, was at the wheel. Guard Clarence Doose, who had also been ordered along on the wild ride, clung precariously to the running board of the big Studebaker. The four prisoners—Straight, Landers, Alexander MacKay, and Joe Kristy—all carried loaded guns, and at that moment none of the captured officials expected to come out of it alive. On a side road some ten miles past San Rafael, Straight looked back and discovered with a curse that they were being followed by Captain Ralph New and several others in a prison car. Indeed, every road in a fifty-mile radius was soon swarming with police cars, and it seemed inevitable that someone would be killed. Straight told Lieutenant Jones to stop and then poked his gun at Doose.

"Get out!" he said.

Doose hopped off the running board and braced himself for the bullet he expected in his back.

"Flag down the prison car," Straight said. "Tell 'em if they don't clear the road we'll kill every man in this car."

Doose obeyed with alacrity, and Captain New held his fire as the big sedan whipped around in a U turn and went back toward the main highway. Still later, as they turned off on another side road toward the Pacific Ocean, the prisoners ejected Mark Noon from the car and also told him to hold off pursuing vehicles which by now were closing in from every possible direction. Near Tomales, a small town on Drake's Bay in a primitive and isolated section of the coast, the car suddenly smacked into a road block set up by a highway patrol posse. The police opened fire without realizing there were hostages in the car, and one of these shots ripped the left rear tire. It exploded with a bang, and Lieutenant Jones fought the drag on the wheel for almost half a mile. Finally the door popped open, the car swerved, and he was flung to the highway. MacKay grabbed the wheel, and the car bumped along on three tires for another four miles until Straight spotted a dairy barn near Valley Ford, some fifty miles from the prison.

MacKay turned sharply off the road, but he couldn't control the car and it plowed into a ditch. Sykes, Atherton, and Stephens scrambled for grass cover, and the four prisoners took refuge inside a barn just as the first of the pursuing posses arrived. MacKay, Kristy, and Landers dropped their weapons and prepared to surrender, but Straight was beyond all reason. He strutted out of the barn with a gun in each hand, and was shot through the head by District Attorney Albert Bagshaw of San Rafael. The other three fugitives surrendered, and the parole board members, two of whom had gunshot wounds in the legs, were hospitalized and later brought back to San Quentin.

It was five o'clock when the three surviving plotters were brought back to tell their story to Julian Alco, then president of the Board of Prison Directors. They confessed that the four automatics had been smuggled into San Quentin under the dashboard of a civilian employee named Harry Simpson. Simpson, who was innocently involved in the plot, lived in San Rafael and drove his car to San Quentin every day. Some weeks before the break an ex-convict named Clyde Stevens, a man long known as a "cop hater," had purchased the guns for his old friend Straight at a San Francisco pawnshop and had secreted them in Simpson's car while it was parked on a San Rafael street. Straight and MacKay removed the guns when Simpson drove into the prison parking area near the garage and hid them in a keg of nails in the carpenter shop.

Just before dinner that evening, while Warden Holohan hovered between life and death, I went back to the office to gather up some of the loose ends. There was one circumstance that mystified me—the prison coats worn by Straight and his gang, and which had been exchanged for the civilian clothes, were not their own. This was easy to prove, because at the time all clothing had each prisoner's serial number plainly stenciled on it. I assumed Straight had previously stolen the coats from other prisoners, perhaps to confuse pursuers. I went to the files to identify the owners, but to my surprise their cards were missing. Then I remembered the four cards I had pulled out that morning for Warden Holohan. They were still on his desk and, as I expected, the serial numbers matched those on the stolen coats. I sent for the four men, talked with them, and was soon convinced that they were not involved in the plot, even though they had not officially reported the loss of their coats. Ordinarily the loss or theft of four cheap coats would not be the concern of the warden's office. But Warden Holohan, like many another prison veteran, often acted on hunches, and he must have suspected that something was brewing. I don't know where he got the tip that morning, or how much he knew. Perhaps the break could have been blocked had he chosen to explain why he wanted those cards. Perhaps not. He never mentioned the subject again, and I don't know the answer to this day. But I have told this story to San Quentin officers many times, saying: "If you hear a rumor, or have a hunch, or suspect something is cooking, don't keep it to yourself. Tell *somebody!*"

Kristy and MacKay, incidentally, were hanged for their part in the kipnaping, but Landers was given a life sentence for his help in preventing the murder of Warden Holohan. Stevens, the handsome thug who supplied the guns, was locked up at Folsom Prison, but he didn't live very long either. He was shot and killed two years later, while trying to break out with six other men in a riot that cost the life of Warden Larkin of Folsom.

Warden Holohan never really recovered from the beating he got that January day.

He came back to work weeks later, to be sure, with the physical scars healed and with a philosophical remark about the few bad apples in every barrel. But his spirit was crushed and he would have resigned right then, as he admitted later, "if it wouldn't look as though I were knuckling to the cons." Eight exhausting years in San Quentin—through one of the most difficult periods in the prison's history—had drained his strength, and he saw no immediate solution to his many administrative problems. I also think that more than anything he was shocked by the fact that he, an essentially fair and kindly man, was the only one so brutally attacked that day.

He was still in this moody state of mind, debating his personal future, when a prisoner came to the office one day with two ten-dollar bills he had found on a workbench inside the walls. The bills looked good, but they were counterfeit, and Warden Holohan promptly gave them to Frank Sykes, who was chairman of the parole board as well as a member of the State Board of Prison Directors. Sykes, intrigued by this unique form of contraband, phoned Captain Thomas B. Foster of the U. S. Secret Service in San Francisco.

"Here's one for the books, Captain," he said. "Somebody smuggled some counterfeit ten-dollar bills into the prison."

"Smuggled in, hell!" said Captain Foster, who is a

forthright man. "Those bills are being smuggled *out* of San Quentin."

"I don't believe it," Sykes protested.

"I don't blame you. You won't believe you've got a counterfeit plant inside the prison, either. But you have."

"But that's fantastic."

"It certainly is. We weren't quite ready to break this case, Mr. Sykes, but under the circumstances we won't wait any longer. I'll send some men over right away."

Two weeks later, to the profound embarrassment of all concerned, the Secret Service broke up one of the most unusual, not to say impudent, counterfeit operations in its history—a plant that was turning out thousands of ten-dollar bills inside San Quentin's walls. The copper plates, paper, inks, aging materials, and finished bills—a neat little layout, paid for, without official knowledge, of course, out of state funds—were all found in the prison photoengraving shop. The brains of the gang was a Los Angeles photographer named Jack Lewis who was doing time for bank robbery. His organization included half a dozen prisoners, four or five parolees who served as passers, and a number of civilians who, unwittingly or not, were taking out packages of counterfeit bills and bringing in the necessary materials. Like all counterfeits, the ten-dollar notes were just fair reproductions, but they might have been better if the artists involved had not been interrupted in their schedule. As it was, the bills were given a fast aging by an inmate named Theodore Gounis. He folded and rubbed them by hand, and steamed them over a bucket of boiling water. Gounis also devised a celluloid mask which he placed over the bills when he was coloring them by hand.

He used a green oil color and laboriously worked it into the paper with a piece of cotton. Lewis had already run off more than twelve thousand dollars' worth of currency, and had enough material on hand for another five thousand notes. After the confessions were signed, Captain Foster admitted a little sheepishly that he had been keeping an eye on San Quentin since the day he discovered in a friendly conversation with Warden Holohan that a new photoengraving plant had been installed at the prison.

"I just felt," he said, "that any time you put a bunch of crooks into the same room with photoengraving equipment, in or out of prison, you're asking for trouble. Sure enough, one of these fellows soon ordered some copper plates in San Francisco, and they were sent to the prison on a state requisition. After that it was only a matter of watching and waiting."

The first counterfeit turned up in Seattle near the home of an ex-prisoner who had worked in the photoengraving shop. The next one was passed in San Rafael—three miles from San Quentin—by another engraver on parole. Fourteen of the notes were found in the San Francisco home of a third ex-convict. All three of these men began to sing when Secret Service agents picked them up, and Captain Foster had been on the verge of "raiding" San Quentin when the spurious notes were found inside the walls. There were a lot of red faces in San Quentin when details of the counterfeit case were revealed in the newspapers, and for a while there was gossip that the prisoners were betting—they'll gamble on almost anything—that certain guards and officials would be fired.

I guess I was the only one in the office not surprised by

this remarkable affair, because counterfeiting in San Quentin was nothing new to me. Years before, when I was in the seventh grade at the little San Quentin school, I delivered newspapers to guards and officials around the prison reservation. Some of my customers paid me promptly, but many others were potential dead beats, and in order to collect I used to hang around the warden's office on payday and grab them as they came out counting the cash in their pay envelopes. More than once they slipped me lead quarters and half dollars, made by the prisoners and given to the guards. I was afraid to take these clinkers home to my mother, who counted on the newspaper collections for our slim family budget, and so I simply passed them along to others. But one day I was caught buying candy with a counterfeit quarter, and I have never forgotten the scolding I got at home. "Clinton," my mother said sternly, "if you don't mend your ways you'll wind up in prison someday." Years later, when I became warden, I reminded my mother that I had certainly tried to mend my ways but that I wound up in prison anyway.

In some ways the counterfeit scandal was the last straw for Jim Holohan. There were some other aspects of it, too, which the public knew nothing about at the time but which worried all of us. We learned from Jack Lewis's confession, for instance, that knockout drops, poison, narcotics, whisky, and other dangerous items were being sold inside the walls to anyone who had the price. Whisky was commanding five dollars a pint, and potassium cyanide for suicide purposes, as Ethan McNabb discovered, was available at a very high price. Lewis told us about one prisoner who had smuggled in a whole pound of chloral hydrate, the chief ingredient of a Mickey Finn, and he had planned to drop some of it into a big coffee kettle used by the guards. Some of these contraband things were coming into the prison disguised as photographic supplies for the engraving shop, and the narcotics apparently were being stolen from the hospital. Lewis further revealed a conspiracy to buy machine guns in San Francisco and ship them to San Quentin hidden in barrels of hypo destined for the photoengraving shop. Confronted with these facts, Warden Holohan felt in his heart that he had been betrayed, not so much by the prisoners, perhaps, but by the lawmakers, the politicians, and the people—those who denied him the men and the money he needed to keep things under control. He resigned a month later and went back to his ranch home in Monterey County after a final and cynical public denunciation of the whole California prison system.

The prison directors immediately replaced him with Court Smith, who was then warden at Folsom. Like Jim Holohan, Smith had been a peace officer in the Western tradition, an ex-sheriff whose six-foot-six frame and two hundred and fifty pounds of muscle had impressed and cowed Folsom's toughest inhabitants for almost nine years. Smith was frankly hard-boiled, and the men of San Quentin were naturally apprehensive about his disciplinary plans. Smith evidently sensed the undercurrent of fear in the prison, and on his first day of office made a reassuring announcement to the press that he would soon abolish San Quentin's medieval and notorious dungeon. Warden Smith may have been sincere at the time, but the fact remains that the dungeon was being used more and more instead of being closed.

I had known about the dungeons since childhood, for my father often talked to us about what he called "the shame of San Quentin." But I had never seen this dreaded subterranean hole until the day I was sent there to interview the occupants for a census report. The dungeon was a black tunnel about fifty feet long, with seven small cells on each side. The ancient mass of rock and concrete had the musty odor of a tomb; no sunlight had touched its moldy walls for almost ninety years, and the foul air had no place to go, for there were no windows and the cell doors were hand-forged iron. Each cell was nothing more than a niche cut into the stone, and the walls and floor were bare. There was no light, no bed, no ventilation, no toilet facilities, not even a bench. There were sometimes three or four men in one cell, and there was no place to sit except a triangular block of concrete in one corner. Prisoners slept on the damp floor, with one blanket if they were lucky, and they got bread and water at the whim of the guards. I had to use a flashlight to take my notes, and for weeks afterward I was haunted by the memory of the shrunken faces I saw in the dim light, the smell of the living dead, the drip-drip of moisture from the vaulted ceiling.

Yet—even if some thought such punishment was justified in extreme cases—not all these men were vicious criminals, not all incorrigible, not all lost souls. Some were shoved into the hole only because they had turned in a poor piece of jute cloth or quarreled with a con boss or wisecracked to a guard. As time went on, while there was much small talk of reforms, the dungeons were filled with forgotten men. There was no appeal from a sentence to the hole, and men who complained were sapped with a rubber hose or whipped by the lash. When there was too much trouble or noise, the dungeon guards would throw lime on the cell floor, wet it with a bucket of water, and wait for the fumes to punish the helpless men inside.

Hate and fear walked hand in hand elsewhere in San Quentin, too, and no one would have believed that this was the same "modern" prison where kindly Jim Johnston had fought against the barbarism of the strait jacket and the striped suit, or where Jim Holohan had tried to give imprisoned men new dignity and inspiration as they paid for their sins. This was a supposedly enlightened age, not much more than ten years ago, but up in the cell blocks— in the row called "Siberia"—men were being forced to stand on a nine-inch circle for hours at a time. If they moved or talked or turned around, they were dragged into a back room and beaten with a hose or leather straps. Prison officials were depriving inmates of decent clothing, blankets, and other simple necessities so they could claim savings for the taxpayers, and the food was often sour or only half cooked.

Like a lot of other workers in San Quentin, my hands were tied. I had been transferred from the warden's staff, of course, when Smith came in with his own secretaries, and had moved over to the parole board, first as historian and record keeper, and later as an assistant to Secretary Mark Noon. I had a wonderful opportunity to watch and work with men who were anxious to earn their paroles, and through them I became aware of the hell bubbling inside the walls. San Quentin trembled on the brink of riot, and we were afraid that if it came, many lives would be lost and prison progress would be turned back a hundred years.

Toward the end of 1938, San Quentin was a city of nightmares, and the growing crisis could no longer be kept secret. John Gee Clark, a Los Angeles lawyer and penologist who has since become a Superior Court judge, had just been appointed chairman of the parole board and was being deluged with unbelievable complaints. Clark quietly began a personal investigation and found many guards, officers, and prisoners who, no longer able to stomach the increasing abuses, talked freely and furnished irrefutable evidence. Clark turned this information over to Governor Culbert Olson and urged prompt action to avoid the inevitable break. "Things are going to get hot around here," Clark told me. "You're on the parole board staff and you'll probably be suspected along with everyone else. I want you to stay out of this. Don't tell me anything. I can get all the information I need."

Not long afterward the whole San Quentin mess was exploded in the newspapers, and Governor Olson ordered open hearings at the prison. He came down from Sacramento to hear the testimony himself, and no punches were pulled as witness after witness told him of the chaos in the big house. Subsequently, after reviewing the evidence, Governor Olson publicly ousted the entire board of prison directors, and on July 13, 1940, a new five-man board convened at San Quentin to consider the next move.

I sat on a long polished bench outside the meeting room for what seemed like hours, mopping my face and listening to a flood of the wildest kind of rumors. Mark Noon had been in and out of the room once or twice, flushed and nervous, and a number of official heads were about to be lopped off. I was sure I was due for the chopping block myself, and had made up my mind to quit prison work for good. Warden Smith was summoned before the new board early in the afternoon, and almost at once loud voices filtered out into the hall. Smith emerged at four o'clock, and clumped down the stairs without a word. He was through—after four years of bloodshed and strife. I was alone on the bench now, and I waited half an hour before someone called out: "Duffy—you're wanted inside."

I walked in and sat down, wiping my glasses to hide my nervousness.

"Duffy . . ." someone said, "we have not agreed on a new warden. You've been around here all your life and you know all the spots. How about taking over for the next thirty days?"

I could have crawled under the rug. "Taking over?" I asked mechanically.

"Yes—as warden."

Warden for thirty days. Warden Clinton T. Duffy. It sounded like a miracle to me. It still does.

3 I was probably the most surprised man in California the day I was named warden at San Quentin, because, like Cinderella, I never expected to be tapped by a magic wand and transported to another world that had seemed so inaccessible most of my life.

Forty years ago, when I was a small boy whose family life was controlled by guns and lockup bells, we lived in a shabby white house just inside the prison's main gate. The house was so small—it would be called a bungalow now—that my four sisters were squeezed into one little bedroom while my two brothers and I had to sleep on couches in the living room. When we were finally able to buy a large bed in which all three of us could sleep, my mother had to put an ironing board between Ray and Bill every night to keep them from fighting. My father was struggling along on fifty dollars a month as a guard, and my mother's main worry was not the hundreds of so-called dangerous men who surrounded us, but the much more urgent problem of caring for nine people crowded into such small quarters. Once during that difficult period my mother was awarded a prize for having the largest family in the county. We were all excited about it, and Mother, wearing her prettiest dress, went down to get the award. It turned out to be a big silver spoon instead of the cash she needed so desperately, but she accepted it with a gracious smile and brought it home as proudly as though it were a Nobel prize.

Like other women raising families in our uneasy little prison town, my mother sometimes looked out her window at the warden's house up the street, not with envy, but with wistful longing for the abundance of its twenty-one rooms and eleven baths. The great Victorian mansion perched on a steep hill behind our house, just as it does today, but it was as remote and austere as a feudal castle, and ordinary people were never invited inside the doors. The formal gardens around the house were forbidden territory for San Quentin children, and we rarely ventured there unless it was on a dare or we were sure the warden wasn't home. Sometimes we sneaked up to the house after dark and stole pomegranates from a gnarled old tree, or wheedled ice cream from the Chinese cooks at the kitchen door. I was often accompanied on these taboo excursions by Gladys, whose father was then just a guard, and sometimes we pretended that I was the warden and she was the warden's wife. In this childhood game we dreamed big dreams, as kids will, and made imaginary changes in the prison rules that would have shocked our parents. As we grew older and went on to high school outside the prison, Gladys and I occasionally talked about what we might do if we lived in the great house on the hill. But we knew it was still only a dream, more unreal than ever, and by the time we were married we had long since come down to earth.

When the state prison directors suddenly accepted the resignation of Warden Court Smith and moved me up from parole board secretary to be acting warden, I was not only incredulous but scared. I came down from the meeting room to the office where Warden Smith was kidding the office staff and giving "farewell" kisses to a couple of newspaperwomen. I think he confidently expected to be reinstated and had no intention of yielding the job to anyone else. It was about six o'clock when I left the building, and I stood outside on the concrete plaza for a moment, gazing up at the familiar mansion on the hill. Nothing was really changed; the vines clung tightly to the prim white walls, and the old-fashioned high windows with their green shades still had the vacant look of a blind man's eyes. The big lone palm tree prodded the skyline like a frazzled mop, and far above its tattered fronds, on the crest of the hill, the guard in Tower 20 fingered a high-powered gun and watched every moving thing. I wondered then if the house would ever be home to Gladys and me.

But that night at least I was warden, and would be for thirty days more. Thirty days, with much to do, and nothing to lose by doing it. While I was musing about these things I suddenly remembered that my niece, Marjorie Duffy, was having a birthday party that night in our little summer cabin at Guernewood Park, a resort town on the Russian River some forty miles north of San Quentin. Gladys and our son Jack were already there, and I had been delegated to bring the cake. I went to a phone and called her.

"I won't be up tonight," I said.

"But, Clint—you promised to bring the cake. Anything wrong?"

"Well, there's a sort of emergency. I . . . I've been appointed warden."

I could hear the wires humming, but Gladys was silent.

"Hello . . ." I said. "Did you hear what I said?"

"Yes . . ."

"Aren't you going to congratulate me?"

"Do you think I should?" she asked.

I had no answer for that. I knew that Gladys was probably a little numbed with the realization that our old way of life was finished and that we had assumed a great responsibility to the people of the state of California and to those thousands of men behind the walls.

"Jack and I are coming home, Clint," she said.

"All right."

I hung up, and walked down San Quentin's long main street to a house close by the gate. I knew the house almost better than my own, for it was there I had courted Gladys. It was there, too, that her father had given me the wisdom of his long years behind the walls and taught me that no one was ever reformed with a whip. But Captain Johnny was dead, and now the house was occupied by Captain Ralph New, under whom guards had used the dungeons, the straps, and the rubber hose so much that they had cost a warden his job. Captain New came to the door when I knocked, and I told him I had just been appointed warden.

"I've heard that," he said shortly.

"All right," I said. "I'm making some changes, and as of this minute, you're through."

I went back to the office, which was deserted by this time, and telephoned Joseph Fletcher, a guard whose work I had watched for many years. "I'm appointing you Captain of the Yard," I said, "and as your first official act you're going to abolish the dungeons." He was startled by the order, perhaps even a little dubious about my authority. But he went inside the prison immediately and closed up the foul fifty-foot cave where hundreds of men had suffered unbelievable tortures through the years. The next day, worried that my order might not stick, I had the heavy iron cell doors ripped from their concrete moorings and dumped on the prison scrap heap. Not long afterward, when war came, the ancient doors were San Quentin's first contribution to the scrap-metal drive. Today the dungeon cells, which were once the shame of our California prison system, serve as a storage room for soft drinks, cigarettes, candy, and other little luxuries, and for the first time in some ninety years there is light and fresh air in the hole.

On Monday, July fifteenth, I went to the office for my first official day as warden. I found Smith was still occupying the warden's office and unwilling to talk with me, and so I had to set up shop at a long table in the waiting room. Almost immediately I was snowed under by a flurry of phone calls, letters, telegrams, requests for personal interviews, and even a few anonymous threats. There was a pile of scrawled notes, many unsigned, tipping me off to things I already knew, and several letters from nervous employees offering to resign. I tossed everything into a file tray for the moment and consulted a memorandum I had scribbled out late the preceding night.

I fired six guards, not only because they had beaten up

prisoners for years at the slightest provocation, but also because I was afraid that sooner or later they might get their throats cut in retaliation. I banned the use of whips, straps, rubber hoses, and all other forms of corporal punishment, and had an inmate painting crew obliterate the nine-inch circles in one of the cell blocks where offending prisoners had been forced to stand for hours at a stretch without moving or talking. I issued an order abolishing head shaving for new prisoners, because I felt that coming to prison was humiliating enough without the added indignity of this medieval practice we had inherited from California's Spanish days.

I signed another order eliminating the big numbers stamped in black on every inmate's clothes. At the time we didn't have enough unmarked shirts to go around, and for quite a while, until the old clothes wore out, we had to paint out the numbers with India ink. This clothes-numbering practice was originally intended to put a convict label on the men so they could be spotted quickly if they escaped, but I had always thought the idea was silly, simply because a fugitive with any sense would shed these telltale clothes as fast as he could. This was clearly demonstrated, for example, in the 1936 attack on Warden Holohan and the kidnaping of the parole board, when the prisoners involved exchanged clothes with their hostages.

There are times now when I wish we could do away with numbers entirely. We rob a man of his identity; we rub out his name and give him a number instead. The number is soon etched into his mind, and he remembers it for the rest of his life. It calls him to the visiting room, it shows up on his mail. It's on his privilege card, and in the books he borrows from the library. He has to use it every day, year in, year out. I knew an old lifer once who was uncomfortable after he went home until his daughter embroidered little tabs with his old number and sewed them to his clothes. I still get letters from former inmates who can't shake the habit of signing the number they had behind the walls.

"Believe me, Warden," one man wrote the other day, "the sweetest sound in the world is not the friendly noise of our neighborhood, or the money rattling around in my jeans for the first time in five years, or even the voices of my kids. It's hearing somebody call me 'Bill' without that damn D-1077." It is a small thing, perhaps, but I like to think that today the men of San Quentin can hold their heads a little higher because, though they are prisoners in every other way, at least they don't have to carry the glaring brand around on their clothes.

Looking back now, I realize that the orders I issued that first morning must have been quite a shock to the old-timers around San Quentin, especially those who still remembered me as just another one of Guard Bill Duffy's noisy kids. I know there was a lot of gossip among the older guards, and I also heard later that some of the employees considered me a meddling amateur who would eventually get his ears pinned back. Indeed, five of these men soon stomped into the office and quit, telling me frankly that I was turning San Quentin into a playground and they didn't want to stick around for the riot. I must admit I didn't urge them to stay, because that day I was much more interested in the reactions of five thousand men who could not march into the warden's office to speak their piece. Shortly before noon I left the office and walked over to the old towered building which serves as a control point for what we loosely call "the inside"—that portion of the prison completely surrounded by high walls. The three-story structure, built of brick and stone blocks almost a century ago, still has the original parapet and high cathedral windows, and looks more like a prison than the big cell blocks that squat around it. A short corridor, with a steel gate at each end, leads through the building to the walled area, and it is here that prisoners who are newsworthy by journalistic standards usually pose for their last picture before they're swallowed up inside. There were half a dozen officers waiting at the first gate when I got there, and I told them I was going into the big yard.

"All right, Warden," one of them said. "These men will go with you."

"No, thanks," I said. "I'm going alone."

"But you can't do that, Warden."

For a moment I thought he was kidding me, so I said, "Why not?"

The officer looked at me with pained surprise. "No warden ever goes into the yard alone," he said. "None of 'em ever have. It's too risky. If you'll excuse me for saying so, Mr. Duffy, you've been around here long enough to know that."

"Well, there's always a first time," I said. "Unlock the gate."

He shrugged, turned away, and looked through a glass observation window in the steel door. Then he twisted a big brass key and let me out reluctantly, muttering that he wouldn't be responsible for my safety. I crossed the prison garden, turned left past the battered Spanish cell block, and soon reached the enormous concrete yard, a quadrangle larger than a football field, formed by three cell blocks and the huge mess hall. Thousands of men swarmed over the stone flats, shifting and turning to loosen the press of bodies, men doing nothing, men going nowhere. Their clothes were shapeless and dirty gray; they walked with a slouch and some talked from the corner of the mouth. I stood there for a moment, watching the gray pattern, the light faces and the darker ones, the tired eyes of the old and the cold eyes of the young. They knew I was there. The news had already swept across the yard, and I could see the solid mass ripple, like water kicked up by the wind.

I walked in among them, and I was thinking of the thousand times I had made this brief journey before, as a youngster with my father, as a warden's secretary, as prison historian and clerk of the parole board. It never occurred to me that it should be any different this day; this was my home, this was my yard, too. I suppose I should have considered that there were men in that yard who would have no use for Clinton Duffy, or any warden; that there were also men who had murdered other men for small change or just for the hell of it. I imagine that there were probably no less than two hundred knives, daggers, blackjacks, or other hidden weapons somewhere in those thousands of pockets and sleeves. I suppose I should have remembered also that I was no longer a clerk, but a man who might be worth kidnaping because he could order gates unlocked and guard fire withheld.

But I wasn't thinking of those things. I saw them not

as strangers or criminals or even numbers on a file card, but as human beings whose virtues and faults I knew better than anyone else, whose case histories I had studied for the parole board, whose wives and mothers and children I had known from many a tearful visit over the years. I have since been told that this was a naïve and dangerous view, but I have walked the yard alone another thousand times or more since then, and nothing has ever happened to change my mind. My mind might be mistaken, but my heart tells me I am safer in San Quentin than most other men are on the streets of their home towns.

I went directly into the mess hall from the yard that first morning, and I waited there as the men shuffled in. Overhead, on the steel catwalks stretching across and around the two-hundred-foot hall, four gun guards marched their restless patrol, prodding the air with their automatic rifles and occasionally calling down a warning to prisoners getting out of line. The guns were not exactly an appetizing influence, and I made a mental note to get rid of them. The food was waiting on the long tables in individual plates, or bowls, but I could see that it was already lukewarm, and it looked like something set out for the dog. I asked the civilian steward what it was.

"Beef stew," he said.

"Any beef in it?"

"Not much," he said with a sly grin. "But you know how it is. Beef costs money."

I couldn't help thinking of the beef stew Mother Duffy used to cook for her boys and girls. Old-fashioned beef stew with dumplings. "Why don't you put dumplings in your stew for a change?" I asked the steward.

"Can't be done," he said.

"Why not?"

"We just don't make 'em, that's all. Never been done."

That word "never" did it. "Tomorrow," I said, "you start having dumplings. And once a week thereafter."

The men got the dumplings, and I soon got a new steward.

I spent a lot of time in the mess hall those first few days, sitting on benches with the inmates and sampling what we call the "main line" meals. I never let the stewards know I was coming, and often I popped into the kitchens to see what was cooking. My interest in the food may have seemed overzealous to some, and irritating to others, but my father and Captain Carpenter had both told me many times that a full and satisfied stomach was the best insurance against a riot. I know from my own experience that this was no hollow maxim, because our family, like others in the prison, once lived in fear for a week during the terrible food riot of 1912. It began on a quiet Sunday, while Charlie White, George Goodrich, and several other San Quentin boys were playing with me near the front gate. The usual signal for the kids to come home for Sunday dinner was the three-thirty lockup bell, but that afternoon it tolled at two o'clock. We scurried home, knowing that something was wrong.

Shortly before two o'clock, revolting against the sour and sometimes spoiled food they were forced to eat, the prisoners had started an uprising of such ominous proportions that a general alarm was sounded throughout the county. The riot began when one man gave the signal by calling out, "Pass the vinegar!" and in an instant the mess hall was a shambles. Plates sailed through the air, tables were wrenched from their bases and smashed, and the roar of angry voices could be heard on the highway two miles away. One group of tough prisoners formed a flying wedge and plowed toward the kitchen to get the chief steward, Frank Moulton, and stuff him into one of the ovens. Instead of running for his life, Moulton grabbed a live-steam hose and four of his cooks sprayed the mob until a small army of guards came to the rescue.

The riot boiled on for hours, and the tattoo of gunfire, as guards picked off running prisoners here and there, terrified the then quiet Marin countryside.

For the next two or three nights, before our parents caught us in the act, we boys sneaked out of the house after dark and climbed the hill behind the warden's house to listen to the screams of the men as they were stripped naked in their cells and battered down with salt water from a fire hose. On the fifth day my father, who had been a mess-hall guard in the thick of the fight, was suddenly appointed steward in Moulton's place. It was a wonderful promotion for him, because among other things it meant we could have inmate help in the house, but my mother was almost in a panic and protested that she would rather have him be a live guard than a dead steward. My father admittedly couldn't boil water, but he had respect for decent food and was convinced—riot or no riot—that the prisoners had a legitimate complaint. He had some new cooks brought in, began serving meals to small groups at a time, and soon the riot ended.

This early riot, which took several lives and did tremendous damage, was almost duplicated in 1937, while I was working for the parole board. The trouble at that time was caused by tainted fish balls; hundreds of men became violently ill, and once again there was fighting in the mess hall, fortunately without bloodshed. Both these rebellions were vivid and unpleasant memories to me, and I was determined to give the men better food even at the cost of other important changes I wanted to make. I brought in a dietitian from San Francisco, planned new menus based on minimum caloric requirements for good health, and installed a crude cafeteria system so the food could be served hot. Almost immediately there was a noticeable drop in prison hospital cases, and production jumped in the jute mill and other prison shops.

Despite the obvious improvement, I still found some officials who were indifferent to the needs of the prisoners and who said, in effect, "They're only convicts, so they're lucky to be eating at all." Even my new and competent steward didn't seem to get the idea. One day—more than a year after he went to work—he came to my office with a sheet of statistics and flourished it under my nose.

"Look, Warden," he beamed, "for the past two months I've saved you better than five thousand a month on your food budget."

"Louie," I said, "if you come back here next month and you've saved me even five hundred dollars—you're fired."

In some ways it was awkward making these drastic changes in the old order while Court Smith was still isolated in the warden's office. He came in every day, just as though he had never been relieved of his duties, and sat at a desk for hours tearing up papers and filling up one wastebasket after another. He was still occupying the warden's house, too, and he did not leave San Quentin for good until President Isaac Pacht, of the prison board, formally ordered him out of the office several weeks later. Meanwhile, however, I kept on functioning from the table in the office waiting room, and something new was started almost every day. I got some inmate plumbers busy and they built fresh-water showers—the first time in the prison's history that the men did not have to bathe in dirty salt water pumped up from San Francisco Bay. I eliminated a long-standing ban against local newspaper subscriptions—at one time censors were even snipping crime items from out-of-state papers—because I knew very well that the inmates got all the news via the grapevine anyway, as fast as it rolled off the presses in San Francisco. I tore up a list of stool pigeons who had had a soft racket for years, spying on friends and enemies alike in exchange for small favors from some officials. I set up a pressing shop in the laundry so the men could have their shirts and pants ironed once in a while. Curiously enough, this order provoked particular resentment in the die-hards, and one of them boiled over.

"Shirts ironed!" he snorted. "Who in hell cares how the cons look? Nobody ever sees 'em."

I picked up some faded prison clothes that looked as though they'd been dried on a corrugated roof. I handed them to him and pointed to a mirror on the wall. "Take off your snappy suit," I said. "Slip these on, then take a good look at yourself." He looked at me sheepishly for a moment, laid the clothes down, and went on with his work. He never squawked about anything again, and he is still with me today.

I must confess that there was a good deal of scornful talk during these preliminary skirmishes about "Duffy, the thirty-day wonder," and I'm sure that I was suspected of trying to make a flash showing so I could keep the job. But the things I did had been on my mind for years, and if any of my actions seemed hasty and perhaps ill-considered, it was only because I thought I would be out at the end of the thirty days and thus fast action was imperative. On the other hand, it wasn't generally known that the prison directors approved every change I made, and of course the inmates themselves were telling each other the new system was too good to last. Indeed, some three thousand of them signed a petition asking the board to give me a permanent appointment, without knowing that the directors had already made their decision.

I survived the thirty-day trial period without any friction, and on September first I was given a four-year appointment. My mother, who did not have very long to live, was so affected that she wept, first with pride and then with sorrow, because my father, who had died years before, could not be there to shake my hand and call me "Warden." My brother Bill wrote me an ebullient and excited note, saying:

Dear Clint:

Well! Do dreams come true? You've out-Algered Horatio. You've out-Merriwelled Frank, and you've made old Nick Carter look like just another flatfoot. When home-

town boy makes good in home town, that's one for the book. It's the real McCoy this time, Warden *Duffy.*

I heard from brother Ray, too, who wrote:

Congratulations on the new job. Maybe we can play Run, Sheep, Run up on the terrace and through the warden's yard, as we used to many years ago. I bet Pop would have been thrilled over your appointment, as all of us are.

A day or so later Warden and Mrs. Smith moved off the reservation, and now, for the first time in years, Gladys and I walked into the hillside mansion without an invitation. We stood in awe at the threshold for a moment, like kids in a haunted house. It was dark in the high-ceilinged hall, and there was very little light coming from the musty old parlor just to the right of the door. We went through the house quietly and dispiritedly. We were vaguely disappointed and a little repelled, because the whole ancient structure had the gloom and threadbare look of an old-fashioned undertaking parlor. All the chairs were upholstered in dark gray or dark green material, .the curtains were a murky velvet, and the rugs seemed impregnated with the grime of a century. All the doors in both wings of the house were equipped with heavy iron bolts, symbols of a fear that lived in the heart of some earlier warden.

"Well," said Gladys, glancing around, "you've got a new job, and I guess I have one too."

"Where do you want to start?" I asked.

"Up there." She pointed to a ponderous brass-and-copper chandelier, made years before by an inmate who must have hated the world. It was ugly and old-fashioned, and it looked as though it might crash any moment. I told Gladys she could do what she wished with it and went back to the office. The chandelier was gone when I came home that evening, and I never saw it again. I suspect Gladys threw it into the bay. Changing other things in that dismal place wasn't quite so easy; it took months of hard work and surpassing patience, but eventually we turned the mausoleum into a cheerful home, and it has never been anything else.

Shortly after we moved into the house I received a heart-warming note from Big Jim Holohan. "I am very much pleased," he wrote, "to hear that your years of service have been rewarded by being appointed warden. Best wishes for a most successful administration." I needed no further encouragement, because Big Jim knew how I felt and what I wanted to do—even though some of my ideas were in strong conflict with his.

I was reminded of Warden Holohan again several days later—this time with something of a shock—when I realized that before long I myself would have to send men to death in the gas chamber. I was warden now; I could no longer "disappear" on execution days, as I often did when I was Holohan's secretary. I knew nothing about the men who were going to die; indeed, I knew very little about the death house itself except that in some ways it was a monument to Holohan's lifelong revulsion for the gallows. He had fought against the rope for years, and had made numerous trips to the state capital pleading for a more decent method by which the state could claim its eye for an eye. He had seen lethal-gas executions in other states and had persuaded Governor Rolph to read a scientific report on the subject prepared in San Francisco by the Society for the Prevention of Cruelty to Animals. The Society offered to demonstrate that lethal gas, while dangerous to use, was "the most humane and quickest, taking but thirty seconds for an animal to become unconscious." I don't know if anyone ever witnessed this demonstration, but the state legislature subsequently passed the lethal-gas law. Governor Rolph had previously vetoed a similar measure after saying that he did not "want to experiment with human misery," but Governor Merriam signed the new bill. Meanwhile, however, Jim Holohan had resigned and was no longer at the prison when the new gas chamber arrived.

I remember seeing the dumpy little riveted steel cell the day it was delivered at the San Quentin docks on a barge. It weighed somewhat over two tons without its grim accessories, and the state paid a Denver firm $5,016.68 for it. Another ten thousand dollars was spent installing the gas chamber in a steel wing attached to the north cell block, and a small pig from the prison farm was the first victim when its infallible efficiency was tested.

I can't help wondering if Jim Holohan, who wisely never came back to San Quentin to see the thing work, ever realized the complex problems involved in generating enough hydrocyanic-acid gas to kill a man. The manual of operations lists twenty-one separate steps for the technical operators alone, and the equipment recommended by the manufacturer and kept on hand includes funnels, rubber gloves, graduates, acid pumps, gas masks, cheesecloth, steel chains, towels, soap, pliers, scissors, fuses, and a mop. The chemical supplies include sodium-cyanide eggs, sulphuric acid, distilled water, and ammonia—with a discount if they're bought in quantity. We pay about fifty cents for a pound of cyanide, enough to execute one man, but other expenses, including the executioner's fifty-dollar fee, the prorated time of the warden, guards, doctors, and technicians, and such things as new clothing for the prisoner to wear for his death, bring the cost of the average execution to one hundred and fifty dollars. Some rabid supporters of capital punishment have thoughtlessly suggested that this is a cheap price compared to the nine hundred dollars a year it costs to maintain each living prisoner in San Quentin, but I have long since concluded that the books will never be balanced on this item.

Capital punishment is a tragic failure, and my heart fights it even as my hand gives the execution signal in the death house. I argued the subject for years with Warden Holohan and others, but was never able to convince them, even when I demonstrated that in one five-year period California police arrested some two thousand men and women for murder but that only forty-six of them were finally put to death at San Quentin. I knew most of these condemned men, and I have officially executed many others since then, but all of them said that the death penalty did not deter them, even momentarily, from committing their crimes.

I remember one in particular, a swarthy young farmer from one of our mountain counties, who not only knew about San Quentin's gas chamber but who borrowed its deadly principle for his own crime. He killed his best friend by generating cyanide fumes in an airtight cabin, and said afterward he thought it was rather a thoughtful way of ending his victim's life. Just a few hours before he was to get a dose of his own medicine, I said to him, "John, didn't you realize that you might have to sit in a gas chamber yourself when you used the cyanide on your friend?"

"Warden," he said, "I never gave it a thought."

More than one newspaperman has told me that murderers are rarely executed, or even sent to Condemned Row, if they have the right connections or enough money to finance the costly legal fight for their lives. This cynical attitude, which is more prevalent than most people realize, further contributes to the futility of the capital punishment law, so that the gas chamber holds terror only for those who are actually strapped into its iron chair. I am sorry to say that many of the thousands of citizens I have conducted through the prison actually enjoy standing around in the death house, and often are bored with any other phase of prison life. Men visitors are generally awed by the cold, surgical neatness of the little green room where the gas chamber squats, and look away self-consciously when we explain how the executioner's lever drops the cyanide into an acid bucket beneath the condemned man's chair. But many women listen with a curious sort of rapture, and scores of them have walked right into the nine-foot chamber itself and sat down in the metal chair "just to see how it feels." The psychologists probably have an interesting explanation for this sort of morbidity, but it continues to surprise and disconcert me. Formerly, most normal prison activities were halted on execution days and men were herded into their cells hours early, where, the public believed, they sulked about man's injustice to man. I abandoned this funereal shutdown long ago, knowing that even if the men of San Quentin are aware of the gas chamber in their midst, they are too concerned with their own problems to worry about the death of one man they never saw or knew.

But there was one prisoner, a handsome young fellow from Sacramento named William G. Smith, who seemed unusually preoccupied with the official machinery of death. When Smith was serving his term for burglary, the gas chamber had not been installed and the old gallows was still being used. Smith used to hang around the furniture factory, which had housed the gallows room for years, and he asked a lot of questions. He learned how the hanging ropes were stretched and hardened with heavy weights, and how condemned men were measured and weighed for the drop. He knew all about San Quentin's famous murderers and how they died, and suggested, in a casual sort of way, that he was not a common burglar but a killer of some note himself. He implied that if the police had been smart they would have had him swinging too, and he knew exactly what he would say as he stood on the trap. He talked about it to other prisoners and finally confided to a cellmate that he had shot a man in Sacramento. The cellmate promptly told a guard. Presently Smith was whisked back to Sacramento, where the police confirmed that he had, in fact, filled a citizen with lead. He was convicted, brought back to San Quentin, and hustled up the thirteen steps to the gallows, where, in stunned silence, he was hanged. The psychiatrists might say Smith was merely a man acting under a compulsion to seek punishment for his crime, thus accounting for his abnormal interest in the noose. That may be true, but around San Quentin we still think of Smith as the man who literally talked himself to death.

I also remember Smith because he was one of two men who complained bitterly that the gallows was kept oiled and painted, even though it had been outlawed, just so they could have the doubtful honor of being the last to die by the rope. This was true, because for some three years we had both the gallows and the gas chamber ready for use if they were needed. The state law provided that murderers who killed prior to the establishment of the lethal-gas law must be hanged, even though the gas chamber was already being used on other condemned men. Smith was one; the other was a man named Raymond Lisemba, who was better known to the public as "Rattlesnake James" because he tried to murder his wife by sticking her foot into a box with a live rattlesnake. She was actually bitten and suffered incredible torture from the poison until Lisemba became impatient and drowned her in his bathtub. The crime was committed on August 5, 1935, but Lisemba managed to drag out his legal fight for seven long years. He was philosophical about his fate, and organized a Bible class on Condemned Row which was instrumental in converting many a godless prisoner to a helpful faith. On May 1, 1942, when I finally led him out of the death cell to the gallows, Lisemba was ready to go. "Warden," he said, "I've been around here a long time and you have treated me with consideration. But I would rather die than spend the rest of my life in prison."

Not long after Lisemba died I asked one of the engineering shop crews to dismantle the scaffold. There was a good deal of personal satisfaction in this order, because to me that skeleton of wood and rope was symbolic of all that is barbaric in man's relation to man. I had always shared Warden Holohan's revulsion for the whole ruthless instrumentality of the rope and, even if men still had to be executed in San Quentin, I was glad that never again would any man suffer the ignominy of a noose around his neck. Apparently I was not alone in the intensity of my feeling, for the night before the crew was to start work a man named John Howard sneaked into the abandoned gallows room with a crowbar. He ripped out the overhead cross timber, which had a groove cut into it from the friction of countless ropes in fifty years. He tore out the painted trap that had dropped out from under 215 black-hooded men and destroyed its steel trigger. He broke up the booth where three guards, hidden from view, used to cut the slim cords that released the trap. He left the crowbar leaning against a wall and went out into the night panting, exhausted, a man who had purged his soul of a long-nursed hate.

I don't know how John Howard got into the gallows chamber without being seen. I never asked him. I didn't care. There are some who wondered why he was not punished; there were and are rules in San Quentin about the willful destruction of state property, and the penalties are severe. But I knew John Howard, and I knew he had already suffered enough. He had come to Condemned Row years before, sentenced to death for a crime in Los Angeles, and the passing weeks brought him nearer and nearer to the end. He lived each day, and died each night, and when the guards came at last it was not to break his neck but to send him back to Los Angeles for another trial. He was returned to San Quentin on a lesser charge, and he vowed that he, and he alone, would destroy the scaffold if the chance ever came. He finally got that chance, and he did what he had to do.

I think Jan Valtin, author of the successful *Out of the Night*, might have shown a similar ferocity if he had been there that night, although he has perhaps mellowed and softened in the twenty years that have passed since he left San Quentin. I knew Valtin as Richard Krebs, then an inflammable and rebellious youth in his early twenties who was serving a term for armed robbery. He had a terrible hunger for knowledge, and he was a prolific writer despite the handicap of being unfamiliar with the English language. Warden Holohan asked me to censor Valtin's stories before they were printed in the San Quentin *Bulletin*, a literary magazine that flourished at the time, and sometimes I had difficulty tempering his explosive phraseology to fit the prison rules. The *Bulletin* offices were in the furniture factory building immediately adjoining the gallows chamber, and on hanging days Valtin and others on the staff were compelled to wait in the big yard until the execution was over. I never discussed capital punishment with Valtin, and it was only recently that I discovered what he thought about it at the time. In a book published after *Out of the Night* he admitted that he had imagined himself in the condemned man's place and that he developed a consuming hatred for "a system in which men could be strangled slowly and with pious serenity." Valtin naturally looked upon condemned men with the eyes of a fellow sufferer, and his out-of-focus admiration turned certain cold-blooded murderers into heroes. I have not seen Valtin since he was paroled and became a successful writer, but I have often wanted to ask him whether he has enlarged his horizons enough to include the men, women, and children who were the victims of his valiant golden calves. I hope he has.

It is probably quite natural for writers who have served a prison term to remember most vividly the cruelties, the sordidness, and the heartaches they saw while they were locked up. When Valtin, for instance, finally got around to discussing his San Quentin experiences, he did it with a cynical indictment against executions, guard brutality, sour food, the prison stench, and all the other miseries he may have suffered. Donald Lowrie's *My Life in Prison,* which was a sensation years ago, had a similar saturation of despair. Jack Black, too, penned *You Can't Win* in jaundiced retrospect. No doubt all these things happened. Some prisoners can deaden their sensibilities even under the worst conditions; others are sickened by the slightest adversity or discomfort. There are also men who have an unlucky genius for making trouble or antagonizing guards and officials, and undoubtedly they get worse treatment than most other men. But as I reread stories written by some of our ex-inmates, even conceding that they are true, I can't help making comparisons between the prison as it is today and the San Quentin of old which had a reputation as one of the most primitive penitentiaries in the world.

When I was a pupil in the San Quentin elementary

school many years ago, we went to our classes in an atmosphere that would have frightened any normal youngster. There were guns everywhere; the guards carried clubs, and the prisoners wore stripes. Shootings, stabbings, and minor revolts were everyday occurrences. But these incidents were never mentioned openly in school, so we would not be frightened, perhaps, and we were not taught anything about the volcanic history of San Quentin. I think we were probably more afraid of John George, a mysterious old Greek fisherman who had a shack outside the walls. John wore earrings made of fish cord, kept his baggy pants up with a rope belt, and killed fish by biting off their heads with his sharp teeth. On Sunday afternoons, when we helped him with his heavy nets, John paid us off with a few fish, or with enchanting legends of the early days, including stories about good St. Quentin and how he performed miracles on that very spot.

It was a long time before I discovered that old John was not only a Munchausen who knew nothing about San Quentin history, but was a ruffian who had done his early training in an Eastern penitentiary. Actually, as I search my memory now, I don't know which was more exciting—John's fables or the true account of the once-dreaded place which has been my home for fifty years.

San Quentin, part of a large Spanish land grant known as the Rancho Punta de Quentin, was not named after St. Quentin at all. The name was borrowed from Quentin, an Indian chief whose tribe lived on the rocky point, and is properly pronounced "Kaynteen," though no one uses this pronunciation today except an occasional tourist. Many inmates simply call their alma mater plain "Q." On July 14,

1852—Bastille Day, appropriately—a slimy, unnamed bark-entine dropped anchor in the mud flats off Point Quentin and became California's first state prison. The barnacled old vessel, owned by the pioneer General Mariana Vallejo and his friend General James Estell, was intended to house forty or fifty men until the first cell block could be built under a lessee arrangement with the state. But before the end of the year the various sheriffs, eager to save their jail space for influential drunks and an occasional useful Deli-lah, began unloading their troublesome prisoners on Estell. Since the sheriffs were allowed to charge one dollar a mile for bringing prisoners, they were also sending along many Mexicans and Indians who were convicted on forgery charges even though they couldn't write their own names. The distance from Los Angeles to San Rafael—as marked on the expense accounts in those days—seems to have been six hundred and sixty miles, but it has shrunk unaccount-ably to four hundred and twenty-five miles since then.

In a few short months the prison ship was a living hell. More than one hundred and fifty men were jammed into its fetid holds, and the guards, they say, stuffed cotton into their nostrils before going below to unlock the cages in the morning. Many of these unfortunates died of disease; others were killed or wounded in fights and attempted escapes. Temporary quarters on the shore relieved some of the congestion, but the first permanent administration building—which still stands—was not completed until 1854. It was known as the "Stone Building," made from rock and bricks by convict labor, and was so solidly built that recently it took us months to chip away the surface so we could give it a coat of cheerful green paint.

The men and women who came to San Quentin in the fifties to expiate their sins were the scum of the seven seas —gamblers from the gold fields, killers from the crowded towns, the courtesans and the swindlers who found a bonanza of their own among the miners who had struck it rich. Some of them suffered shocking tortures in the crude prison, including thumb-stretching and terrible beatings, and supplies were so meager that less-favored prisoners had no underwear and wore burlap bags on their feet. During the first year alone some eighty-three prisoners escaped, killing or maiming guards in their flight, and most of them took refuge in the thick forests at the foot of Mount Tamalpais. They pillaged farms and ambushed unwary travelers along the dusty roads, and no sensible citizen could be persuaded to invest in Marin County real estate. Nowadays, when the gray spume drifts out of the winter sky and I hear the foghorns bleating like lost calves, I think of poor General Estell's letter to the Marin people, pleading for understanding:

Since the first of January, 98 convicts have escaped. Quite a number have been killed in attempts to suppress revolts and in efforts to retake those who had escaped. At the time this contract was made, it was not contemplated that there would be more than fifty prisoners at any one time, for many years to come. Instead of fifty, there are this day over three hundred . . . Thus situated, we are in the most imminent danger. I have the mortification daily of seeing the graves of my brave guards, murdered by the hands of infamy, and meeting others maimed for life in the discharge of their unenviable duty. . . .

Dense fogs prevail for five months in the year . . .
They are precipitated without notice on the eastern slope,
rendering it impossible to distinguish an object a few yards
off. Prisoners learn all the peculiarities of location and are
not slow in availing themselves of every opportunity. On
one occasion the prisoners passed an entire week in their
cells without being able to go to their meals, the fog being
so dense that I would not risk them out of the prison.

During these fogs the powder and caps are all damp,
and the guns as well, all of which is as well known to the
convicts as to the guards. Consequently there is at such
times greater danger of an émeute [uprising].

Estell probably had some reason for complaint, as I
know from personal experience, but unfortunately he
didn't tell the whole story. Governor Bigler sent investi-
gators to San Quentin, and before long the state legislature
was clucking over a report of such scandalous proportions
that it started a whole new era in our prison history. The
agents said, among other things, that three pretty women
prisoners, known as Scotch Mary, Russian Kate, and Dolores, were dispensing amatory favors like gamblers turning up cards. Two deputy wardens were getting most of
the loving aces, with the result that they carried guns and
threatened to kill each other over Scotch Mary. Kate and
Dolores were snuggling with certain prisoners who had
cash resources, and liquor was available day or night to
any prisoner who could pay for it. Prisoners were allowed
to roam around the county at will; some were even permitted to act as guards, and a sober officer was apparently

considered a freak. Escapes were a daily event, and gambling games were open to all comers around the clock.

The lawmakers pretended to be abused, but were seriously disturbed only by the numerous escapes and the fact that the prisoners were not doing enough work to earn their keep. The lusty code of the gold-rush days was reflected by their attitude toward the availability of liquor at San Quentin. Why, they asked, should these unfortunates, deprived of their liberty, also be deprived of the staff of life? Nevertheless, to save face, they broke Estell's lease and replaced him with a new board of prison directors.

In the turbulent twenty-five years that followed, San Quentin became a political toy that was soon shabby and unwanted. Graft and blackmail were openly tolerated. Estell regained his lease after the state had lost thousands of dollars operating the prison, and finally sublet it to a clever scoundrel named John McCauley. He ran the prison like a feudal empire until October 1860, when the state reluctantly bought him out for $275,000 and sent in Lieutenant Governor I. N. Quinn as ex-officio warden. The next four years under Quinn and his successor, T. N. Machin, were the bloodiest and blackest in the shameful narrative of San Quentin. Prisoners were treated like animals; half their hair was shaved off and they wore tattered clothes with horizontal stripes. Men were cut to ribbons with whips if there was the merest suspicion that they planned an escape, and discipline was enforced with the horror known as the "water cure." Prisoners who could take twenty lashes on their bare backs with a defiant laugh cracked up quickly when the guards sprayed their nose and mouth with the asphyxiating high-pressure hose.

In April 1864 the tortured convicts revolted, grabbed Machin, and prodded him out the gate with needle-point knives against his neck. They went about two miles to a place then called Ross Landing, where they unexpectedly encountered a small army of farmers and wood choppers carrying pitchforks, clubs, and rifles. In San Rafael, where horsemen brought news of the break, panic-stricken householders rushed to the adobe courthouse with their personal treasures, and another group barricaded themselves in the Solomon Bear store. But the convicts lost the battle of Ross Landing; an uncounted number were slain outright, others ran into the hills trailing blood, and those who were captured soon regretted their temerity in the agony of punishment inflicted by the infuriated Machin.

When I hear people discussing San Quentin's modern "tough guys," I am tempted to say that they are Sunday-school angels compared to the rugged men and women who lived through the barbaric genesis of the prison. There was Piute George, who scalped a dozen people and was shot to death in prison; Indian Dick White Rock, who didn't get a life sentence until his third murder conviction; Trency Marshall, who slugged dozens of young men and sold them into slavery from her infamous "Shanghai House" in San Francisco; Modesta Avila, a pretty girl who was a professional train wrecker; Ah Gow, the Chinese hatchet man who was caught in the tunnels beneath San Francisco's Chinatown after his fifth murder; Eben Gubdill, who fed a belligerent sailor to the sharks and eventually won a pardon from President Grant; Gallopin' Johnny Haley, who pulled thirty-eight daylight robberies before he was caught; and the immortal Black Bart, poet of the highwaymen. Many of these and other villains were locked up with a penal program that became more and more inhumane, but they survived to win their freedom.

San Quentin's first full-time warden, J. P. Ames, took over the prison in 1880. He was followed by Paul Shirley and John McComb, Jr., but none of these three accomplished much in the way of reform, despite the crusading efforts of kindly John Wilkins, a new member of the prison board. Wilkins was fifty years ahead of his time, and was ridiculed and condemned for his compassion especially because he asked the state to furnish the prisoners with socks and underwear.

It is hard [he wrote after retiring] to understand the bitterness of the public against any intelligent measure of prison reform. The whole attitude was one of uncompromising vengeance against criminals.

Granting of credits upon good conduct aroused the wrath of the state. An earnest protest was raised when the whipping post was abolished. Men who had given the subject of penology painstaking study were denounced as maudlin sentimentalists. To propose an appropriation for better conditions was to receive a prompt rebuke from the solons, and draw down on one's head a perfect avalanche of hostile criticism.

The man who had received a jolt of several years in the degenerating atmosphere of San Quentin . . . found himself a pariah against whom avenues of respectable employment were closed. He was dogged by the officers of the law, and if by some chance he secured employment under an alias, his former record was inevitably revealed.

93

Only a resolute, capable swimmer kept his head against the adverse current.

The parole law was passed and approved [in 1893] before the public and the press understood its real purport. When they realized the meaning of its text, the law was forcefully denounced as a scheme for wholesale jail delivery.

In 1918, when Wilkins wrote this impassioned account of the not-so-gay nineties, he believed that San Quentin had since become a haven of mercy and that the twentieth century had brought an enlightened public opinion to support that policy. But the perfect prison still does not exist anywhere, nor does complete public understanding. I doubt that it ever will. And I am sufficiently dubious about human nature to expect too much from the public. Too many people are still hypocritical about criminals. I recall one prominent clubwoman who shrilly demanded imprisonment for her neighbor's son when he was involved in a scrape with a girl. "That boy's no good," she said. "He should be locked up for good." Two years later, when her own son was convicted of a crime and sent to San Quentin, she came sobbing into my office. "Society is responsible for this," she said. "It wasn't my boy's fault. Please be kind to him and help me get him home soon."

The urgent need for public understanding of the crime problem and our program in the new San Quentin is one reason why I have encouraged representative groups of citizens from every section of California to visit us and see prison life at first hand. I only wish that each of them could complete this research by spending a few nights in a cell, taking orders from officers, marching to meals, and answering to a number instead of a name. In this connection I am reminded of Asa Keyes, a man who learned, too late in life, what it means to live in prison. Keyes was the swaggering, ruthless district attorney of Los Angeles who rarely lost a case and who seemed to prosecute every offender as though it were a sacred duty to put him behind bars. Keyes sent a total of four thousand men into San Quentin, and dozens to the gallows. One day, with dramatic suddenness, he was caught taking a bribe, and presently found himself a manacled passenger on the prison train from Los Angeles to San Quentin.

Warden Holohan and I were truly afraid for Keyes, because more than a third of all the men then in San Quentin had been prosecuted by him. We decided to give him an office job, where he could not mingle with other inmates, but Keyes had courage and insisted that he wanted to know the victims of his zeal. Within six months Keyes had hundreds of new friends, and he was generous with legal advice for those who couldn't afford a lawyer. He was a new man, with unwonted wisdom and compassion, when he finally got a parole, and he promised to spend his remaining years helping other men in trouble.

"Prison doesn't help any man," he said the day he left. "It's a poison, degrading all but the strongest. I don't know what to substitute for penitentiaries, but if I were district attorney again, I would hesitate about sending so many men to prison. It is far more terrible than people realize, and the sentences are too severe."

Subsequently Keyes was granted a gubernatorial pardon and made plans to open an office in Los Angeles. But the excitement and the strain were too much and he dropped dead two months later. This was unfortunate in more ways than one, because Keyes would have made a very vocal and sincere ambassador for the cause of modern penology. I was particularly impressed with what he said about the uselessness of prison terms for most men, because not long afterward thirty American prison wardens, polled by an Eastern jurist, reached a similar conclusion. I personally believe that prisons with walls and cells and guns are necessary for a great proportion of our so-called criminals. For some first offenders twenty-four hours in San Quentin would be—and is—a nightmare, and is thus a sufficient deterrent. For others the critical point comes in a month, or a year, or years. But there is a saturation point in practically every man's servitude beyond which every additional hour is wasted and destructive punishment. Occasionally men who are locked up too long become "stir simple." We have them in San Quentin, men who could have been salvaged ten or twenty years ago, when the scars of their crimes—they're not all murderers, either— were still raw and painful. But there is no hope of rehabilitating them now, and they will be a public charge as long as they live.

4   "Warden," the condemned man said, "what happens tomorrow . . . after I . . ."

I knew what he meant. He was trying to say "after I die." He was wondering whether someone would come for him after the execution, so he would not have to lie in the crude San Quentin cemetery, with nothing but a numbered stick over his grave. I have been asked that last-minute question before, but I have rarely had the heart to give a direct answer, especially when I know in advance that no one will claim the body.

"Now don't worry," I said. "Everything is arranged for. Everything will be the way you want it."

He gave me a strange, fixed smile. "Yes—I know all that, Warden. But what I also want to say is—where do I go when it's over? I mean . . . is there a life after death? The men on the Row talk about it all the time. What do you think?"

He said it as casually as though he was asking about the weather, but I knew he was strung up like a bow. The death-cell guard turned away in embarrassment, and at that moment the greenish glare of the newly painted steel walls seemed almost indecent. Life after death? What do you tell a man who has only twelve hours to live, a man whose thinking is already in a characteristic state of shock, a sort of twilight zone of distorted movement and shadow talk? What do you tell a man who has no God, a man without a church who has turned the prison chaplains away? I knew he was not afraid, as most men understand fear, because death is a welcome friend when you have already died a thousand deaths in the cat-and-mouse play of the law—the endless writs, appeals, petitions, and reprieves. His fear was of the unknown, and so I told him, as I have since told many others, to search for the answer in his heart and in his mind, and that there he would find whatever he wished.

Perhaps that was a wrong and hollow answer. Perhaps it was an evasion. I don't know. But he believed me because in that hour there was no other belief for him. I watched him die in the gas chamber the next morning, and I could see that during the long night he had found an intangible something to give him strength for the coming darkness. He nodded to me through the thick observation window, his lips formed the word "okay," and he was smiling.

That afternoon, as is our custom following an execution, Gladys and I drove aimlessly down a country road south of San Francisco, trying to get as far away from the gas chamber as we could. I suppose I am only fooling myself in these temporary escapes, because I know I have to go back, and there will be another execution, and another. Indeed, some of my friends in the prison world have chided me for running away those few hours, on the grounds that emotion is not a proper part of a warden's job. They may be right, but I have never been able to shut my mind to the personal problems of my men, especially those I must put to death. And that evening, long after we came back to San Quentin, I could still see the dead man's pale, sagging face, and I knew there was a new stick on the bare and dusty graveyard hill. I wonder what he found.

This incident was still fresh in my mind a few days later when I received word that Thomas McMonigle wanted to see me in Condemned Row about something "very urgent." McMonigle was a tall, husky, shaggy-haired hospital orderly who had been sentenced to death—with considerable attention from the press—for the kidnaping and murder of a Santa Clara County high-school girl named Thora Chamberlain. McMonigle was a disturbing and potentially dangerous influence on the Row because the other men didn't like his boast—and unfortunately it was true—that he had hidden the girl's body so successfully that the police never found it. I distrusted McMonigle's behavior, mostly because he kept taunting the officials merely to get his name into the papers, and I had been personally tricked by his pretended willingness to reveal the location of the grave. Once we let him out on a court order so he could show Santa Clara County deputies the exact spot, and he had insisted that I go along.

"Warden," he said, "you've got to be there, because when we find the body one of these cops will put a bullet through the girl's head and then claim that's how they found her. They never had a thing on me."

I humored him because I thought it might persuade

him to talk, and we started out in a state car driven by Tom Cheetham, who was then my executive secretary and is now a guard captain. We rode around the thickly wooded Santa Cruz mountains and along the Pacific Ocean for more than two hours while McMonigle eagerly gave directions. Late in the afternoon, as we passed an abandoned quarry, he yelled: "Stop! This is the place. You'll find her down there." We parked the car, took our handcuffed prisoner with us, and scrambled down into the rubble of stone. But there was no body. "Well," McMonigle said with pretended ruefulness, "mebbe I picked the wrong place today. Next time I'll remember where it is sure enough and mebbe you can bring the newspaper boys along."

As far as I was concerned, there wouldn't be any next time, and when McMonigle sent for me I hoped that this time he would tell us the truth about his victim. I walked across the big yard, took the elevator to the top floor of the north cell block, and went down to McMonigle's cell at the far end of Condemned Row. He jumped up from his cot, obviously excited, and greeted me with an expansive smile.

"Warden," he said, "I want to ask you—what happens after the execution?"

I couldn't have been more startled if he had reached through the bars and slugged me. I decided immediately that somehow the grapevine had picked up my conversation in the death house the week before and that McMonigle was baiting me.

"What do you mean?" I asked warily.

"After I'm dead," he said, peering at me with his frosty blue eyes, "my body belongs to me or whoever claims it. Ain't that so?"

"I suppose it is."

"And if a guy wants to bring me back to life, that's okay too, huh?"

I looked at him closely, but there wasn't a flicker on his broad face. I had seen other men lose their minds on the Row when the clock began to cut them down, but McMonigle's execution day was weeks off, and there had been nothing significant in his regular medical reports.

"You feel all right, Mac?" I asked.

"Why, sure, Warden. You prob'ly think I'm kiddin', but I ain't. I know a guy who can do it. He's got a machine that'll bring me out of it after I get the gas."

"All right, all right," I said soothingly. I was sure now that his mind was at least temporarily unbalanced and that a psychiatric examination was in order. I told McMonigle I'd think it over and let him know. The following morning I was visited by Dr. Robert Cornish, a Berkeley scientist who had achieved considerable notoriety some years before with an involved method of bringing dogs back to life after he killed them in his laboratory. Dr. Cornish frankly admitted that he had a similar plan for reviving McMonigle after the execution and was convinced it would be as successful as it had been with the dogs.

I was so intrigued by his proposal that I played along with it for quite a while, but soon realized that he and McMonigle were serious and fully intended to carry out the experiment. Dr. Cornish wanted to take McMonigle's body from the gas chamber as soon as the prison physician pronounced him dead. He planned to inject antidotes, stimulants, and other fluids directly into the veins, and to place McMonigle's body into a machine that would set the blood in motion and eventually induce a heartbeat.

101

"Doctor," I said, "can't you find a subject somewhere else, maybe a carbon-monoxide victim?"

"I've tried half a dozen times," he said, "but I can never get to them soon enough. I must have the body immediately."

I told him he would have exactly the same problem in the gas chamber, because McMonigle's body would have to remain there at least an hour. The concentration of hydrocyanic gas in that small space is so dense, and so terribly dangerous, that powerful blowers are kept running for half an hour to pump it out, and at the same time the chamber and its apparatus are neutralized with ammonia. There is another half-hour safety period after that, and even then the men who remove the prisoner's body wear gas masks and rubber gloves. "The only way you can do this," I said a little impatiently, "is for you to sit alongside McMonigle in the other chair, so you'll be handy."

"Maybe I will at that," he snapped.

Dr. Cornish went away in a huff, and I thought that would put an end to this grim fantasy. But when the courts denied McMonigle's appeal and set the execution for February 20, 1948, Dr. Cornish called at my office twice more, demanding a chance to try his invention. I had to tell him quite bluntly that I wouldn't discuss it again without orders from some higher authority. I told McMonigle, too, as gently as I could, that he could not be a guinea pig. He brooded about it for days, and finally, in a gesture of revengeful whimsey, insisted that I invite his ex-wife, as well as a former sweetheart, to watch him die. Very few condemned men know that the law allows them to invite any five witnesses they choose. McMonigle not only knew it, but perversely forced me to send out those two letters. I had never allowed women to attend an execution, but in this case I would have had no choice. I kept a nervous eye on the witnesses as they gathered outside the death house just before ten o'clock, but fortunately the two women did not come. McMonigle floated into the gas chamber like a fish in a tank, sobbing and hopefully searching the audience for a familiar face, and he was so confused that he almost sat down in the wrong chair. I remained a little longer than usual that morning, but nothing went wrong, and Thomas McMonigle stayed dead. I've often wondered if he *could* have been brought back.

I never think of the McMonigle affair without remembering Leslie Gireth, who really wanted to die.

Gireth was a jeweler in the city of Glendale, an attractive, successful young man with a pretty wife, two children, and a fine reputation in his community. Sometime during the summer of 1941, Gireth met a girl named Dorena Hammer, hired her for his store, and before very long was taking her on week-end trips. About a year later Gireth and Dorena went on a long trip north to Alameda County, across the bay from San Francisco, and registered in an auto court. Toward dawn of their first night there, Gireth quietly placed a gun against the sleeping girl's head, pulled the trigger, then went out and telephoned the police. He had a portable phonograph and was playing Debussy's "Clair de Lune" in the cottage when the officers arrived. Gireth coolly refused legal advice, pleaded guilty, and was sentenced to death.

I talked with him many times on the Row—about the war, Glendale, his family, prisons, music, art, and other things about which he had considerable knowledge, but when I asked him about the girl he would turn away and say nothing more. This sparring went on for months, but Gireth refused to reveal why he murdered the girl or why he would not fight for his life.

"I came here to die, Warden," he said, "and I would like your promise that you will do nothing to help me get any stays."

"I don't understand that, Leslie," I said. "You're the first man in San Quentin history who doesn't want to live."

"I can't expect you to understand," he said softly. "I hardly understand it myself. I can only say this—I have an appointment and I will keep it."

I took him down to the death cell one Thursday night —it was in January 1943—and he asked me if he could have the phonograph which had been taken away when he entered San Quentin. I gave it to him, along with the Debussy record, and left him alone with the deathwatch. Later in the evening I went back and found him lying dreamily on the mattress in the cell, listening to the music and puffing on a cigarette.

"Leslie," I said, "there isn't much time. Is there anything special you'd like?"

"Well, yes, there is," he said. "Would it be too much trouble to get me two hamburgers and two cokes?"

I told him that was easy. He might have asked for roast pheasant or some other delicacy because of the popular misconception that condemned men can order anything they want for that last meal. As a matter of fact, many people still believe in that overworked phrase, "the condemned man ate a hearty breakfast," but actually only one man in ten has any real appetite when his life is running out, and at San Quentin we can only offer them what is available. It so happened that we had no hamburger buns that night, but Gladys drove into San Rafael and was able to find some in an all-night grocery. We took six Coca-Colas out of our own refrigerator, put them in a basket with half a dozen hamburgers, and sent them to the death house. The next morning, just before the hour, I noticed that Gireth had consumed only two sandwiches and two of the bottled drinks.

"Thanks for sending all that food, Warden," he said in an apologetic tone, "but I really wanted only two. You see, whenever Dorena and I went anywhere—to the beach, or on a picnic, even the night she died—we always had a hamburger and a coke and our own little phonograph. And last night, well . . . it was just the same as always. Thanks so much, and good-by."

He shook my hand, stroked his hair into place, threw back his shoulders, and walked steadily through the chamber door. Shortly afterward I found a note in the death cell, perhaps the most remarkable letter I have ever received. It was hand-lettered in a fine engraver's script, on an engraved letterhead with the Gireth family coat of arms, as follows:

My dear Mr. Duffy:
There are times when one can say very little, but these few words I mean in all sincerity: Thank you so much for everything.

Leslie B. Gireth

A day or two later a package came to the house from Glendale, and in it was an expensive Japanese silver cigarette case, "With the compliments of Leslie Gireth." It was a lovely farewell gift, but after seven years it's still a mystery to me. Leslie Gireth knew that I never smoke.

Perhaps someday we will know more about Gireth's crime, and why he did not try to save himself. Apparently it was an impulse murder, and it is conceivable that a competent attorney could have gotten him off with a life sentence. The average lifer in California serves about fifteen years, and Gireth would still have been young enough to start afresh. It has been suggested that he, a man with an unblemished personal record, was so overwhelmed with guilt feelings when he realized what he had done to his family that he saw no other atonement except the penance of death for himself and Dorena Hammer. Or perhaps it was a suicide pact, with Leslie lacking the nerve to carry out his end of the bargain and deciding to let the state do it for him. I cannot pretend to analyze the psychological motives involved in the case, but I suspect that Gireth would have been miserably unhappy as a lifer and very likely would have killed himself.

It seems to me that I have been acutely aware of San Quentin's Condemned Row, like a sore that refuses to heal, as far back as I can remember. It probably began in the little San Quentin schoolhouse, where an eccentric teacher named Miss Redmond took a sadistic pleasure in arousing her pupils to the horror of the gallows. On execution mornings she was pale and tremulous, and would usually make the grave announcement that a man was about to be hanged. "In that building right over there," she would hiss ominously, pointing to the brick furniture factory. "Just think of it, children, that poor man . . ." It was never news to us, of course. Every San Quentin youngster knew the meaning of the deathly stillness that fell upon Prison Town on those gloomy Friday mornings. Those of us whose fathers were assigned to duty in or around the gallows building were especially disturbed, and even under ordinary conditions we would have found it difficult to concentrate on our schoolwork. But Miss Redmond wasn't satisfied with that. Shortly before ten o'clock, as the death march began, she would put down her book and say: "Oh, children . . . that poor man has only fifteen more minutes to live." She had an old-fashioned pocket watch on her desk, and sometimes I can still hear it, ticking away in that hushed room. "Now it's only ten minutes . . ." she would whisper. She had learned somewhere that it took between ten and fifteen minutes for a man to die on the rope, and she had it timed in her own mind until at last she could groan: "There . . . it's done . . . he's dying . . . dying . . ." And while a man was dying and a woman with a twisted mind extracted a perverted pleasure from it, fifteen or twenty small boys and girls were being scarred with psychological wounds that few of them ever forgot. Miss Redmond's peculiarities were eventually unmasked, and she was replaced, but the damage had been done. Later, as a boy tagging along through the prison garden after my father, I used to look with awe on the impregnable, whitewashed Spanish cell block where the condemned men lived, and once in a while, if the light was right, I could see pasty faces pressed against the small slot in the iron doors, trying to see that incongruous patch of roses below. The cells were nothing more than stone boxes, without much air or light or sanitary facilities. They were built in a dark age, almost a hundred years ago, when no one cared what happened to the highwaymen and the thugs who came to California to pillage the gold seekers, and who were sent to the state's first prison. Like many another guard opposed to treating men like animals, my father had a contempt for that cold heap of stone and sorrow for the prisoners inside, men who were virtually forgotten until it was their time to be hanged. But there was not much one man could do about it, because tradition was not treated lightly in those days, and by tradition the living condemned men were already as good as dead.

The men sensed the atmosphere of hopelessness, too, and suicide attempts were frequent. Many of the men I visited for Warden Holohan told me quite bluntly that they would end their own lives—if they could manage it— and we had to watch them day and night. But a few succeeded, including a burly miner named William Kogut. I had talked with Kogut several times about his appeal, and about the friends from his home town of Oroville who were trying to save his life, and I thought he would hold out until the last minute. But one October night, when vigilance was momentarily relaxed, he removed one of the hollow iron legs from his bed and stuffed it with torn-up playing cards. He had soaked the cards in water until they were a sticky mass, and after he filled the pipe he sealed the two ends with pieces of wood from a broom handle. About three o'clock in the morning he laid the pipe on the oil heater in the cell, held his head close to it, and waited for results. The crude bomb exploded with a concussion that jarred other condemned men in their bunks and woke up almost every prisoner in San Quentin. Kogut was whisked to the hospital, and Dr. Stanley tried to save him, but he never regained consciousness. Later, probing the damaged brain, Dr. Stanley plucked out a portion of a card that had been driven several inches deep. It was the ace of spades.

The condemned men were finally given a row of new cells in the big north cell block, but even with this change the old attitude of indifference was still apparent just before I became warden. I was anxious to do something about the Row right away, but I was so involved in the general prison reorganization that it was some time before I could get up there for a complete checkup. My first two executions, which occurred only a month or so after I took office, seem blurred in my memory now, probably because I did not know the men, and also because I was no longer a mere spectator, but the man who had to order the cyanide dropped. I remember one of those two, a handsome twenty-one-year-old boy named Rodney Greig, only because the newspapers called him the "vampire killer." He didn't look much like a vampire to me when he was strapped into the chair, but more like a scared kid who never did understand why he stuck a knife into his girl.

Shortly after the Greig execution I made a number of changes in the Condemned Row rules, and we have been gradually improving conditions there ever since. In the old days, for instance, the men were allowed out of their cells for "exercise" for only one hour a day. This exercise generally consisted of walking, back and forth liked caged creatures, under the watchful eye of the gun guards, and most of them were glad to creep back to the solitude of their holes. I added an extra hour to the so-called recreation period, and gave the men unobstructed use of a long, light, and airy corridor where they can walk, play softball, checkers, or quoits, sing, play musical instruments, or just talk. Once they even used the hall as a stage while competing in a prison quiz show against a team from another cell block. In that match, by the way, the condemned team of five made a shambles of the opposition, but they never had a second opportunity to show their intelligence. They are all dead now.

The men are now permitted to write and receive an unlimited number of letters, where formerly there were restrictions on the amount of mail allowed, and a typewriter from the warehouse stores department has been put into an empty "office" cell on the Row where it's available to all. That typewriter caused some raised eyebrows, and there were dire predictions that it would be ripped apart in a week and that some of its sharp rods and bars might be found sticking out of someone's back. But after all these months the typewriter is still intact. It is beginning to show wear, to be sure, but only because of the millions of words ground out of it in the desperate fight of the condemned— the writs and briefs, the frantic appeals for mercy, the fumbling letters to the loved ones who are the real victims of lethal gas.

Illiterate Tex Thompson, one of the Alcatraz Prison rioters, for instance, is one man who could really have used the typewriter. I can still see him perspiring over complicated legal phrases from his lawbooks, laboriously translating the words with a dictionary, and trying to write his own appeal to the Supreme Court of the United States.

Thompson and Sam Shookley, another Alcatraz rioter, were board-and-room prisoners at San Quentin; that is, the federal government rented two of the Condemned Row cells for $3.25 a day each, including meals, and later paid the state three hundred dollars for the use of the two gas-chamber chairs. Thompson, who never finished the third grade, used to tell me he would beat the big rap, and he tried for almost two years. He went without sleep during his last forty-eight hours of life, and was still scribbling away when they came to take him down for that last, short stretch to the chair. Ruthless and violent all his life, Thompson was a good loser nevertheless, and his last request reflected an admirable sense of humor. He had spent all his money, about one hundred dollars, on his now use-less lawbooks, and just before the end he turned them over to me. "I've learned a lot," he said, "and I'd like to give these to some guy who really needs 'em. Send 'em to my lawyer."

In Condemned Row, one of the loneliest and most de-pressing places on earth, humor like this is as rare as rain on the desert and just as welcome. There is often some prankster and wisecracker on the Row; I have known some who spent all their waking hours cooking up gags, and I have seen others enter the gas chamber laughing, as though death were an enormous joke. The psychologists might say that laughter among doomed men is only a shield for their fear, but this is a generalization that would not apply, for example, to Wilson de la Roi, a young French-American we had on the Row. He came to us from Folsom Prison, where he had been convicted of attacking and killing a fellow prisoner, and for the next four years, in between laughs, he fought for his life because he said he liked to befuddle the "mouthpieces." He kept himself busy drawing florid greeting cards for me and Mrs. Duffy, or for some friends, or conceiving practical jokes which may or may not be funny by professional standards but which certainly amused his companions on the Row. He would send notes to the music department, among others, and ask them to dedicate numbers to the boys on the Row, such as, "I Want a Pardon for Daddy," or "I'll Be Glad When You're Dead, You Rascal You." These songs invariably got a chuckle along that corridor of gloom, and De la Roi would roar with the rest. "Why, I'm just like a surgeon, Warden," he said. "I keep 'em in stitches. Hah hah."

De la Roi survived the cruel suspense of eleven reprieves but was finally turned down in October 1946. I was afraid he might crack when he realized that things weren't funny any more, but I was never more wrong. I was standing by his cell one evening when he was only hours from extinction and I said, "Wilson, are you sure there's nothing more you want done?" He looked at me gravely, and his voice dropped to a whisper. "Yeah, Warden," he said, "I'd like a little bicarb because I'm afraid I'm gonna get gas on my stomach tomorrow." Before I could recover from the shock, the Row guards came to measure him for the new clothes he would wear to his death, and he was still snickering when I turned away and went on to another cell.

We had another character on the Row for some time, a Los Angeles factory worker who called himself John Peterson because he said he got writer's cramp using his real name, which was Jan Sarazzawski. Peterson would grow a beard one week, then shave off half of it with the explanation that he was the original "Mad Russian," and furthermore, he said, the razor blades we supplied were too dull. He was only kidding, of course, but about that time a friend donated an electric razor for the condemned men—we couldn't buy them with state funds—and Peterson used it regularly thereafter. He rewarded me with a bombardment of cartoons, which he showed first to his pals for a laugh, in which he pictured himself dangling from a gallows rope or squirming in the fatal chair. He often represented me in these sketches as a bald or toothless warden who really enjoyed executions, and he spent his last hours entertaining me and the guards, or so he thought, with one dirty story after another.

But how little we know what is really in a man's heart. There might have been twenty John Petersons in San Quentin, but I did not discover until after the execution that it was he, the ribald, callous killer, who had long been sending sentimental little poems, thoughts, and greeting cards to my wife because her voice, heard on the prison network, reminded him of someone he had lost in the long-ago.

I sometimes talk about De la Roi and Peterson when I come across a broken spirit on the Row, or I read the men a poem that was handed to me by another jester on the threshold of death. It goes like this:

> *"If I could have my last wish,"*
> *Said the prisoner one day,*
> *As they led him from the death cell*
> *To the chair not far away,*

"Please grant me this request, sir,
Ere you tighten up the strap,
Just tell the Warden I would love
To hold him on my lap."

I suppose it's obvious why this little verse usually lightens their blues, and I enjoy reading it as much as anyone else. There's another classic San Quentin story in this vein which also tickles the men. It concerns Lew Ayres, the motion-picture actor, who came to visit San Quentin one day and accompanied me to the old factory where we had the gallows room. As I opened the door of the high-ceilinged room, with its blue walls and the complicated scaffolding of twin gallows and dangling ropes, Ayres gave it a quick and admiring glance. "Oh look," he said innocently, "a gymnasium!"

The remark seemed funny to me at the time, and still does, but it also planted an idea in my mind. Why not build a gymnasium there? I couldn't do anything at the time, but after "Rattlesnake James" was hanged and the gallows was removed, I had the room repainted and remodeled. We installed a boxing ring, lifting weights, punching bags, and other equipment, and now, after half a century of association with death, the big hall is bringing pleasure and a healthier life to hundreds of men during their idle evening hours and on week ends.

But unfortunately, as long as the people want capital punishment, there will always be a place like the Row, a corner for outcasts, where even gay guitar music played by a prisoner has a haunting sadness and the fresh flowers

Gladys sends down from her garden seem to wilt too soon. For despite all the small things we have tried to do to help the men forget, the Row remains essentially what it is—a straight line of thirty-four 10½ by 4½ foot steel-and-concrete cells within steel-and-concrete walls, shut off from all the sounds and sights of San Quentin, locked and interlocked, rimmed by a steel cage and armed guards and watched every minute night and day. And on the Row everyone talks and thinks of impending death because they cannot escape their thoughts, nor the evidence that they are marked for a special fate. They wear slippers instead of shoes, and their meals are served on trays from a steam-table cart. They're allowed to keep leftovers and snacks, but only in shatterproof plastic jars, and a missing knife or fork is instant cause for a shakedown. They are the only prisoners with bathrobes, but the robes have no belts, and when they take showers in an empty cell used for that purpose, someone watches every move. And always there are those dreaded Thursday nights when one of them is hustled out of his cell, steered to a small elevator with his wrists bound in leather and steel, and taken directly down to the death house, five stories below.

I have seen this scene depicted dramatically in many a movie and once or twice on the stage, but these re-enactments are almost never true to life. It may be a depressing commentary on human nature, but almost every man on Condemned Row believes that he, alone, will be saved. He worries only about himself, rarely takes an interest in the other fellow's case, and does not want to be reminded that a man is actually on the way to death. So there are very

115

few emotional farewells or tears, and, as in the other cell blocks of San Quentin, the passing of a human life is no more than a brief shadow on the sun.

Once in a while, under the pressure of a tremendous fear, a condemned man loses his mind just before execution time. The California law holds that no man can be put to death unless he knows why his life is being taken and understands the difference between right and wrong. In short, he must be legally sane. There is a grim sort of irony in this stipulation, because during those last dreadful hours of suspense the responsibility for gauging a man's mind and his thoughts lies with me. How can I know when a man is insane? Is he insane because he will not eat or sleep or because he talks hysterically? Is he insane because he behaves strangely in the face of death? I don't know.

Not so very long ago I had an emergency call from Officer F. W. McNeil on Condemned Row. He asked me to come there at once. "One of the men just tried to kill himself, Warden," he said.

I left the house and went up to the Row with Dr. Stanley and Charlie White, the boyhood friend who is now my administrative assistant. In one of the cells we found the sprawled figure of a young man named Erwin Walker, a swarthy, handsome ex-army officer who had been sentenced to death for killing a state policeman some months before. Walker was in a coma; he had a paper bag jammed down over his face and a radio earphone cord was noosed around his neck. He was barely breathing, and there was a queer blank look in his eyes when we took off his crude mask. The doctors worked on him and quieted him with a shot of morphine.

"What happened?" I asked Officer McNeil.

"Well, Warden, he had a bad night. Didn't sleep much. He knew he was going down to the death cell tonight. Just a little while ago we heard a funny noise in his cell and we saw him trying to strangle himself with this cord."

I shook Walker gently and spoke to him. He shrank from my touch and stared at me, but there was no recognition in his eyes. He seemed to be in a state of profound shock; his lips moved but made no sound. The doctors thought he might snap out of it, but I wasn't so sure. I stayed in his cell for half an hour and then returned to my office, deeply disturbed. Once, long years before, a man had been carried to the gallows strapped to a board that helped stiffen his spine. I never forgot that scene, and I prayed that I would never have to supervise such an ordeal myself. I hoped that Walker was malingering and that before nightfall he would respond and realize that the punishment was inevitable. Indeed, I was somewhat surprised at Walker's collapse, because I knew a good deal about his case. Walker was at the California Institute of Technology when the war broke out, a brilliant student with a special talent for electronics. He went overseas as an army lieutenant in charge of a radar maintenance crew, and fought with distinction. Returning to California as a hero, Walker suddenly became morose and unpleasant. He puzzled his family with frequent secretive and nocturnal prowls on which he usually carried a machine gun, and he talked mysteriously about a radar gun with which he intended to attack the United States government.

Unknown to his parents, he began breaking into shops

and stores and stealing an amazing and, as he admitted later, "silly variety" of items—carbon rods, textbooks, microphones, motion-picture equipment, folding chairs, tools, an adding machine, and many other things for which he had no use. He drove a car equipped with electronic devices, burglar tools, and nitroglycerin, and he was never without pistols and a submachine gun.

One night in June 1946 he was stopped outside a Los Angeles meat market by a state highway patrolman and former Folsom Prison guard named Loren Roosevelt and asked to show some identification. Walker whipped out an automatic—he has since said he felt he was "a zombie floating in a sort of fog"—and killed the officer with a point-blank shot. Six months later, after a prolonged spree of car thefts and holdups, Walker was captured in a gun fight with the Los Angeles police. The details of Walker's criminal career were so unusual and dramatic that they were made into a motion picture called *He Walked By Night*. By a curious coincidence, this film was playing in some of our Marin County theaters about the time we were making preparations to execute Walker, but I don't think he ever realized that his crimes had achieved this sort of dubious immortality. He never mentioned the picture; he was concerned only with the much more real life-or-death crisis of his own. Eventually the courts turned down all Walker's appeals, and his father, crushed by the costly and futile fight for his son's life, committed suicide.

None of us suspected that Walker might also try to kill himself; he always seemed so cool and detached, and I felt that he would keep the tradition of the condemned. But he was not faking, as it developed, and when I returned to the Row that afternoon he was still incoherent. We helped him make a fumbling change into the new clothing he would wear for the execution, and almost had to carry him to the elevator for the short trip down to the death cell. Hours later his condition was unchanged, and I decided I could not take the sole responsibility for the state of his mind. I telephoned Dr. Leo Stanley and Dr. David Schmidt, chief psychiatrist for San Quentin, and asked them to examine Walker. The next morning, with the official witnesses waiting outside the gas chamber and the executioner standing by, seven consulting psychiatrists crowded into the little death cell to look at a broken shell of a man. Walker was mumbling to himself, crawling like a whipped dog on the floor, and hiding his head under a blanket. At intervals he burst into tears, and jumped wildly at the slightest touch. The doctors were unable to make him talk, and at 10 A.M., the hour set for Walker's death, they signed a statement declaring that he had gone insane. I canceled the execution immediately, the first time in my memory that a condemned man had been saved at the last minute because his mind had snapped. Several days later Erwin Walker was formally found insane in the Superior Court at San Rafael and was transferred from San Quentin to the Mendocino State Hospital in northern California.

Unfortunately, that was not the end of the story.

Walker was given electric-shock treatments, and slowly the once sharp mind began to respond. Six months after his arrival at the hospital he was rational enough to engage in a remarkable verbal duel with Dr. Schmidt and six other psychiatrists who examined him, and some of his answers were highly illuminating. Here, for example, are verbatim excerpts from that portion of the interview which dealt with his suicide attempt:

Q. Have you sort of given up, or are you still willing to battle for your life legally? You haven't given up hope?

A. No, I am still hoping.

Q. Where there is life there is hope?

A. Yes . . . but I don't . . .

Q. You haven't contemplated any means of suicide?

A. No.

Q. You don't plan on any such activity, do you?

A. Not as long as there is hope, no.

Q. Do you know what that would mean to your mother?

A. I have talked to her about that . . . but I haven't any decisions on it . . .

Q. You think it would be more honorable to take your own life than to have the state take it in a legal manner?

A. Well . . . I didn't want . . . I thought it would be better on the family not to have me executed for a crime . . . suicide sounds a little better, I thought.

Q. Was that a true and conscientious attempt at suicide you made on Condemned Row with the radio cord and the paper bag?

A. No, that was something I had planned about a week previously, and I waited until the last possible minute and I went ahead with it . . .

Q. Following that attempt at suicide, what do you remember? Do you remember Warden Duffy coming to see you?

A. No.

Q. Do you remember the warden taking you downstairs to the death cell?

A. No . . . the only recollection I have is being dressed . . .

Q. You don't remember being in the death cell at all?

A. No . . . I thought I was in the psychiatric ward there.

Q. You want to tell us anything more about why you attempted suicide?

A. Well, I think another reason is a resentment—oh, I know I committed all these things, but I don't feel that I did . . . I feel like I'm being punished for a crime for somebody else. I know that is not true, but I have that feeling, and I think I would take my own life to thwart what I term illegal punishment. It isn't illegal . . . but in my mind it is.

Q. It would be a miscarriage of justice?

A. No, I have made my own bed in that case, but I still can't get over this feeling that I would rather take my own life than be executed.

The doctors concluded unanimously that although Walker had shown remarkable improvement, he was still suffering from dementia praecox and needed further treatment. Someday soon Erwin Walker will be questioned again, and then, perhaps, the doctors will tell him that he is cured and that he can go "home," like any other normal patient. And where is home? To him it is the death cell in

San Quentin, for the law says that if he regains his sanity, he must be brought back to die. Will his mind crack up again . . . and again? I wonder.

I think the only time that an execution ever affected the men on the Row, and, indeed, the whole prison population, was the day the Duchess came to die. The Duchess, whose full name was Evileta Juanita Spinelli, was a scrawny, myopic widow whose long, pointed nose and big ears made me think of an enormous mouse wearing glasses. The Duchess, as she was known to her gang of thugs and thieves, was tougher and more cold-blooded than most of the gangsters I've known. She was an expert wrestler, could split a poker chip with a knife at twenty-five feet, and was the mastermind of a mob that specialized in stick-ups, drunk-rolling, hijacking, and, as a curious side line, the manufacture of blackjacks. The Duchess was sentenced to death for feeding knockout drops to Robert Sherrard, a backsliding member of her gang, and then drowning him in the Sacramento River. There has certainly never been a more savage and unwholesome woman criminal in California history, but the news that she was coming to San Quentin to be gassed precipitated a curious wave of grumbling and unrest.

No woman had ever been legally executed in California, and, whether through a misguided chivalry or the urge for a grandstand play, more than a hundred inmates signed a protest and offered to die in her place. These men seriously proposed to draw lots to see which one would save the Duchess, and I had some difficulty explaining why it couldn't be done. I have since concluded that there would have been great consternation, and a fine scramble for the door, if I had suddenly said: "Okay, pick your man." The Duchess, arriving by car from the women's prison at Tehachapi in southern California, thought the idea was a lot of nonsense herself, and was ready to make her exit in the best gangster tradition.

The following morning, while the Duchess was being dressed for her last walk, I had a phone call from the attorney general's office advising me that her attorney had filed a last-minute writ with the State Supreme Court. While the Duchess was smiling smugly about this dramatic delay, I called Acting Chief Justice John W. Shenk and asked him about the writ. "It has just been denied," he said. "As far as this court is concerned, you may proceed."

It was already twenty minutes past the scheduled execution hour. I had taken my place near the executioner's lever and I nodded to the guards to start the death march. The Duchess swept in dry-eyed, in a new green dress and with a silk handkerchief crushed in one hand. At that critical instant I noticed that there were no witnesses in the observation room. I had to stop the procession, something that had never happened in San Quentin before, and I touched her arm.

"I'm sorry," I said. "Please wait where you are."

"Okay," she said.

It took almost forty-five seconds to round up the twelve official witnesses and fifty-five other spectators, all of whom had been ushered outside when the writ was filed. But that remarkable woman stood there facing the open chamber door, stiff and silent as a fence post, until I told her to go ahead. But I would like to have heard what the undertaker said later, when he found those small pictures taped to her skin just over the heart. Photographs of herself with the mob, or some gangster sweetheart, perhaps? No—just her three kids, and one tiny baby she had seen for the last and only time a week before—her first grandson.

I doubt very much whether anyone thought the State of California had done a noble deed in snuffing out Evileta Spinelli, as cruel and cold as she was. I think Tom Cameron of the Los Angeles *Times* said it trenchantly when he wrote: "The 66 watchers of the Duchess' last act can never be quite the same. They're older, wiser, sadder and, somehow, just a little ashamed." I know that I personally hoped I would never have to execute another woman, but perhaps I was asking too much of human nature, for it did happen again. And this time the victim was someone I knew.

Years ago, when I was working for Warden Holohan, he called me into the office one day and said, "Clint, Louise Peete is beefing about something. Go see her, would you? I don't think she wants to talk to me."

I walked down along the water front past the north block to the impressive four-story building—it is now the San Quentin hospital—where the women prisoners were housed at the time. I sent for Mrs. Peete, talked with her for a while, and discovered, as Warden Holohan suspected, that her grievances were petty and not worth troubling the staff about. I think she was lonely and wanted sympathetic attention from a man. She also took advantage of her position as one of the "first ladies" of San Quentin, a woman who had bathed in the hot tears of the sob sisters and found it refreshing.

Louise Peete, who had really earned the sobriquet "The Enigma Woman," was then in her early forties, a mysterious contradiction in the sisterhood of Jezebels. Brown-haired, slightly plump, and with a complexion like a doll, Mrs. Peete was attractive in a comfortable, maternal sort of way. She had a sweet, shy little smile, an altogether charming frankness in her gray eyes, and her voice was soft and soothing. She looked like all the Mother's Day posters ever painted—but she had a heart like an ice cube. Louise Peete was doing life in San Quentin for putting a bullet into the back of Jacob Denton, a wealthy mining man whose home she had leased in Los Angeles. She didn't do it for love, either; she wanted his car, his bank account, and his home, and she killed him to get them. She laid him out in his own basement, covered him with eighteen inches of good topsoil, and went about her business. Four months later, while she still occupied the house, Denton's body was found by police investigating his disappearance, and Louise was convicted of the crime.

In San Quentin she was querulous about only one thing—her innocence. Frequently she wept that Jake Denton was still alive somewhere and would come back to identify the body found in his basement. But neither the police nor the parole board ever doubted her guilt, and, if the truth were known, a good many people were just a little shivery in the presence of this benign little woman who seemed to have a personal rapport with death. Her first husband, Henry Bosley, killed himself a scant three years after their marriage in Boston. Richard Peete, who married Louise in Denver, and who suffered agonies while she was on trial for the Denton murder, couldn't stand the shock of her sentence and committed suicide in Tucson. The records also revealed that a Dallas hotel clerk who had been friendly with Louise was found dead one day with a bullet in his head, an apparent suicide.

I chatted with Louise Peete many times, but I never dreamed that her homicidal box score was still incomplete, or that I would see her years later under much more unhappy circumstances. In the fall of 1933, when the new women's prison was completed at Tehachapi, high in the mountains of southern California,ʼ the women prisoners were moved out of San Quentin. I was assigned to direct the transfer of the last group, which included all the ladies who had formidable scrapbooks of their infamy, or, as the guards used to say, the "hot shots." Louise Peete, more excited than I had ever seen her, was one. Another was Clara Phillips, the so-called "Tiger Woman," who wasn't a tigress at all and who has since earned her way back into society. Erna Janoschek was there too; Erna, the odd "jazz age" girl who strangled a baby she had been hired to protect. In fact, it was Erna who complicated this risky transfer, because Warden Holohan had a confidential tip that her friends planned to snatch her at the railroad station.

I would have been willing to believe an escape plot involving the beautiful Clara, or even motherly Louise Peete, but I was very skeptical that anyone would want the giggling, snub-nosed girl with the baby face. Nevertheless, we took precautions and asked the Richmond police to form a solid guard line from the prison van to the barred Pullman cars. We put the women into a big bus, boarded a ferry at Point San Quentin, and arrived at Richmond, on the opposite side of San Francisco Bay, in

126

less than half an hour. We hustled our charges into the train without incident, changed to a bus at the small village of Tehachapi, and by nightfall they were in their new home, now known as the California Institution for Women. I said good-by to them all, including Mrs. Peete, and wished them luck.

"Thanks for that, Mr. Duffy," she said. "But you will never see me again—at least not in your neighborhood."

"I hope not, Mrs. Peete," I said.

Ten years passed. I never heard from Louise Peete again, and I was so busy starting my wardenship at San Quentin that I was hardly aware that she had been paroled after serving eighteen years of her life sentence. She was released in 1939 under the name of Anna B. Lee, and went to live with a Mrs. Latham, a parole board investigator and one of her old friends. Six months later Mrs. Latham suddenly became ill, went to a hospital, and died. Mrs. Latham's death was attributed to natural causes, and there seems to be nothing in the record to indicate otherwise. But those who knew Louise Peete convinced themselves that she diffused a sinister aura that was fatal to anyone enveloped in it. This theory might not stand up under the cold appraisal of science, but in retrospect the superstitious bystanders were not far wrong.

Mrs. Peete went to Santa Monica in 1943, after Mrs. Latham's death, and moved in with Arthur and Margaret Logan, personal friends who had helped with her parole application. She married Lee Judson, an elderly bank clerk, and settled down to enjoy life. In less than a year this strange creature with the rosy cheeks and soft white hands murdered Margaret Logan and buried her in a homemade grave, maneuvered Arthur Logan into an insane asylum where he conveniently died, and broke her new husband's heart and life. Crushed with shame when he found that his quaint little wife was not Anna Lee, but the notorious Louise Peete repeating criminal history, Judson jumped to death from the thirteenth floor of a Los Angeles hotel.

"Yes, I dug Margaret's grave," Louise had said. "It seemed like hours and hours. I ruined my hands."

She was swiftly convicted and sentenced to death, and they took her to Tehachapi to wait. The execution was set for April 11, 1947, and the day before, I sent a San Quentin car to pick her up. We had heard through one source or another that Mrs. Peete might attempt escape or suicide; indeed, the matrons at Tehachapi had found a contraband razor blade in her belongings and they were sure she had intended to use it. I could not imagine Mrs. Peete permitting her ego to consider self-destruction. I also think she was not convinced that the state really meant to take her life and expected the governor to rescue her at the last minute. However, I couldn't read her mind, and I ordered her handcuffed for the 350-mile ride from Tehachapi to San Quentin. She was furious, and for the first time in her life publicly revealed the kind of cold rage that must have seized her when she was in a murdering mood.

"I have never been so insulted in my life," she said to Associate Warden H. O. Teets, whom I had assigned to make the trip. "Take these things off my wrists."

"When you leave here," she was told, "you are no longer our prisoner. Warden Duffy ordered the handcuffs."

"Oh, he did, did he?" she snapped. "I'll certainly tell him a thing or two. Imagine! Louise Peete treated like an ordinary criminal."

She was still fuming when the car arrived at San Quentin, and she greeted me with a gush of abuse for what I had done to her, "an old friend." In some ways her rage was a good thing for us both—it was an anesthetic of sorts that numbed her mind for the thing that was coming, and it delayed the painful conversation I would have to have with her about the execution procedure. While she was en route to San Quentin, I had had an inmate crew cover up the gas chamber with huge sheets of canvas. I knew she would have to walk right past the chamber on her way to the death cell, and I didn't want her to face the ugly instrument until the last moment. Actually, I suppose, Louise Peete could have gazed at the gas chamber with much more equanimity than I, and perhaps she would have made some gay comment about the soothing green color of the walls. There has certainly never been a more unruffled victim in that house of tragedy, and it shows in her last photograph. She was wearing a pretty white silk blouse, her brown hair was neatly coiffured, and there was a half-smile on her full lips. She looked like someone presiding at a Parent-Teachers meeting, except for the small placard around her neck with the prison number—35692-A.

I went back to see her early in the evening, and again at midnight. We talked for a long time about a woman we both admired, Matron Josephine Jackson, and about the "old days" at San Quentin. Mrs. Peete recalled with a snicker how, one Christmas Eve, she put her sister prisoners in stitches by singing a parody of the song "My Little Gray Home in the West."

"It makes me sad to remember that," she said softly.

"Of course it does," I said.

"Oh, I don't mean what you might think," she said quickly. "It's sad because they are doing this to me, and I am innocent. If these people want my life, there isn't much I can do about it—but it's wrong."

It was late when I said good night, and she assured me she would sleep. She was fumbling with the dial of a small radio as I closed the iron door behind me, and the muted beat of a blues song followed me into the night. As I went past the reception room, a hundred feet north of the death house, I saw a San Francisco *Examiner* reporter huddled on a bench by the door.

"What are you doing up so late?" I asked.

"I'm covering the Peete story," he said.

"But there's no need to stay around tonight. Why don't you come up to the house and get some sleep?"

"Thanks," he said, "but I have to stick here. The city desk expects some trouble because you're executing a woman."

"Trouble?"

"Yeah. We hear the inmates are gonna raise hell."

"Look," I said, "I was up on Condemned Row this afternoon. There are twenty men there in the same fix, and not one of them even asked me about Louise Peete. There won't be any trouble over this tonight or any other night. These fellows have their own problems and, I'm sorry to say, they won't lose any sleep over her."

The reporter was unconvinced, and I went home

without him. He was still there the next morning, bleary-eyed and vaguely disappointed because nothing had happened. I dreaded the dawn of that day, but I underestimated the chilled veins of Louise Peete, and I found her in a placid, resigned mood. She was waiting in the cell, clear-eyed, with her pudgy little hands folded, and that curious shadow of a smile.

"Let's go, Warden," she said.

We went. It was over quickly.

A week later I had a letter from a woman I will call Mrs. Verna Foster, the only known human being who mourned the passing of the ill-starred murderess. She had sat through the long night at our home, waiting for the execution, because she felt that Louise should have a friend near by in her last hour and also because she had promised to claim the body. Mrs. Foster sat in our home, sobbing quietly just before the cyanide dropped, but afterward she had a snack and a cup of coffee and said she felt better.

Dear Mr. Duffy [her letter read],

One week ago today I stood by the little grave and said good-by. My undertaker, who took care of the body so lovingly, was deeply impressed and would love to meet you someday. I told him how kind you were to me and Mrs. Peete, and he said: "What a wonderful man. I would love to meet him someday."

I acknowledged the note and thanked her, but added that I was not especially anxious to meet Louise Peete's undertaker. Mrs. Foster probably doesn't realize how lucky she was not to become better acquainted with a mortician herself, because when Louise took a fancy to people and turned on her charm, it was the prelude to sudden death. I think she was the only prisoner I ever knew who really could have made me afraid.

5 One afternoon many years ago, when I was a boy growing up behind the walls of San Quentin, I sneaked up the hill behind the warden's house to watch a big brush fire. I had been forbidden to go there because there were prisoners fighting the blaze under the nervous gaze of armed guards, and also for the more practical reason that my mother was afraid I might burn my new school suit. Toward dusk that day, when I sauntered nonchalantly through the back-yard gate, my mother met me with folded arms and an accusing eye.

"Clinton," she said coldly, "you disobeyed me and went to that fire."

"No, I didn't, Mom," I said. "That's just a rumor you heard on the grapevine."

"Oh, it's just a rumor, is it?" she mocked. "It must be a pretty hot one, because it's smoking. Take a look at yourself, young man."

I took a look, and I knew I was sunk. My pants were on fire. The moral of this quick knockout probably escaped me at the time, but it was brought back nostalgically after

I was named warden. Shortly after I took office I started walking through the big yard alone two or three times a week, because I wanted to see for myself what was going on and I wanted the men to have confidence in me and to know that I didn't intend to move around the prison trailed by three or four bodyguards. I also got into the habit of carrying pencil and paper in my pocket—I still do it today—and if some of the men had urgent personal problems, I jotted down the information and handled the matter myself. I kept all officers, guards, and inmates advised of every change in the prison rules—and there were plenty—and tried to anticipate their questions. Nevertheless, the grapevine throbbed with weird gossip about my plans, and if some of the rumors weren't actually smoking, they were hot enough to cause unrest and interfere with the normal prison routine. I decided that the obvious answer, if we could swing it, would be a regular prison newspaper.

Prior to the time I became warden, San Quentin had been without such a paper. There was, in earlier years, a literary magazine called the San Quentin *Bulletin*, and many a prison writer first broke into print on its pages. In some ways the *Bulletin* was the personal plaything of the prison intellectuals, and it gave a number of men an outlet for esoteric fiction which probably could not have been sold commercially. The publication consequently had a limited appeal, was expensive, and was finally dropped.

Two other wardens, both baseball fans, had permitted the occasional printing of a small sports sheet, but it didn't have the little items of inside news that were almost as important to the men as letters from home. What was the new parole policy? When would the prison camps open? What could be sent from home? What about visits from their loved ones? How much tobacco was allowed? These and a hundred similar questions were being answered by cell-block oracles who claimed to have a private line right into my office. Further, many old-timers clung stubbornly to the idea that in prison you had to whisper everything, even the time of day, and were frankly skeptical when I said that as long as I was warden there would be no more secrets in San Quentin. There were also some doubters among the older employees, and when they heard about the proposed newspaper they said derisively that half the prisoners couldn't read and the other half would fill the news columns with coded messages for their pals on the outside. This was sheer twaddle, of course, and I went right ahead with the plan.

Toward the end of November, with the help of several former newspapermen who were doing time, an artist, a make-up man, and the inmate workers in the prison print shop, we were ready to publish. The first edition of the San Quentin *News*, hand-set and printed on gaudy green paper, was published December 10, 1940. The paper was not exactly a sensation, but it was a revelation to the permanent tenants who thought they had seen everything in prison. Those first issues were tough in spots, full of slang and even a little bawdy at times. We printed poetry, quizzes, cartoons, short stories, gags, and news. The letters-to-the-editor column, among other things, was a safety valve for all sorts of wacky stories and jokes, and we printed a lot of curious trivia simply because it raised the spirit of the men. One of these stories, which I like to read to an outside audience occasionally, was called "The First Offender," and, I think, is a light but effective one-minute sermon for any free man who tends to be smug because he has never been in trouble with the police. The story reads as follows:

After diligent research we have discovered that there is no such thing as a First Offender—anywhere. The explanation is quite simple: When you were an infant in the crib, you yelled and disturbed the entire household. That's disorderly conduct.

At the age of five you stealthily made your way into the kitchen and stole some jam while your mother was occupied elsewhere. That's petty larceny.

As a boy of ten you played hooky from school to go fishing and wrote an excuse to the teacher, signing your father's name. That's forgery.

Reaching manhood, you married, and at the church you promised to love and cherish. That's perjury.

You kept quarreling with your wife until you burned her up. That's arson.

After your divorce, you kept out of trouble until you were forty and then you married a girl of nineteen. Shame on you, cradle snatching that way. That's kipnaping.

But the pay-off comes when you sit out in the yard and have the gall to tell your bored audience that you are here on a bum rap. That's murder!

There was one character, the *News* reported, who kept demanding roller skates to get around the big furniture factory. Another seriously wanted to bring in snakes to frighten the sea gulls away. There was the inevitable story about the elimination of the pole vault from the San Quentin track meet, for obvious reasons, and one about the ping-pong players whose balls were wafted over the high wall by the wind and used as clay pigeons by the gun guards. There was the true account of an inmate who listed his occupation as "burglar" on the file card and refused to change it, on the grounds that it was a respectable profession. There was a quaint story about Professor Giovanni, a vaudeville performer who came to San Quentin as a guest entertainer and beat our best pickpockets at their own trade. There was also a straight feature called "The Warden's Column—Facts, Not Rumors." Mrs. Duffy says she always suspected I had a suppressed desire to be a columnist, but she thinks I should have started on some other paper, where the editors could throw out my stuff if it wasn't good. Now, she says, I will never know. Good or bad—I think the column has done what I intended it to do—give facts, not rumors, to the men confined. For the past nine years I have called the shots as I saw them. I have tried not to preach or moralize, but I have offered information and advice, and if it has helped one man to be a better citizen, I couldn't ask for more.

Over the years the poems and sentimental ramblings of some of our *News* writers occasionally got a little sticky, but that was not surprising in this town of lonely men, where anything beyond the stony horizon has the deceptive enchantment of a dream. But these sugary contributions were more than offset by prison wags who brought laughter into dull routine and created legends which, though corny, showed that the men could kid the world, themselves, and their predicament. Thus they wrote of Pickpocket Joe, promising the parole board he'd wear boxing gloves every day if they would only let him out; Second-story Eddie, telling the warden a blackjack is better than a rod because there are no moving parts to jam; Crowbar Jeff, who couldn't break the habit and jimmied his own front door; Creepy Slim, who always thinks he's in a car pool when he wakes up in the patrol wagon; Sleepwalker Charlie, who was cured after he banged his head against the cell bars for the fifteenth time; and Willie the Weeper, the man with the crying towel who symbolizes the summed-up woes of men behind bars. These were the Paul Bunyans and the Johnny Appleseeds of prison lore, and occasionally they got a little boisterous in print. But even a prison paper must grow, and in time they and their picturesque language were crowded out by more important things.

In earlier years prison slang was quite prevalent, and I compiled a glossary of several hundred of the most commonly used words and phrases. But it was an argot more or less peculiar to San Quentin, and many a transfer from some other prison felt the need of an interpreter. Even the late Warden Lewis E. Lawes, who prided himself on his knowledge of underworld talk, was baffled by the yard chatter when he visited San Quentin during the war, particularly by the word "bonaru." It is used in no other penitentiary; it means good, or excellent—i.e., a bonaru job— but even the unofficial prison historians know nothing of its origin. There are probably a dozen or two slang words which can still be heard every day somewhere in the prison, but on the whole the men are getting away from the caricature talk now found mainly in the movies or the crime novels.

Today the San Quentin *News* is an eight-page journal dignified and matured by almost ten years of steady progress, and it has subscribers in all forty-eight states and in many countries around the world. From time to time we have had Walter Winchell, Eleanor Roosevelt, Mae West, and other oddly assorted contributors, and I shamelessly asked Billy Rose to send us his column gratis—which he was glad to do—because the men just didn't have enough cash for the usual charge. The original type fonts have long since been replaced by linotype machines, bought by the inmates from their Welfare Fund, and many of the paper's artists, editors, and writers have made good outside. The *News* now prints some eight thousand copies twice a month, which we claim is the largest sure-fire small-town circulation in the world, because our readers get the paper whether they like it or not, and no copies are lost in the bushes around the front porch. I wish we could say "advertisers please note," but of course we don't carry any advertising, although one retired prowler insisted we should at least have a "Bargain Counter" where our reformed graduates could dispose of their used burglar tools, gats, phony checkbooks, and molls.

I think it is indicative that one of our most popular features today is a scholarly book-review column written by a former university professor who is serving a long term and using the time to share his knowledge with the men. The professor's reviews were recently published in a one-hundred-page book by the prison print shop, with an encouraging foreword by Joseph Henry Jackson, author and distinguished book critic of the San Francisco *Chronicle*.

A typical oversimplification is the public's notion of what life in a large prison is like [*Jackson wrote*]. *Because attention has been focused on the work convicts must perform and on their purely recreational activities, very few have any idea that there is such a thing as intellectual exercise in prison, too, or that there is any opportunity for such exercise.*

Jackson, I think, was understandably surprised that groups of inmates are able to meet in San Quentin for the sole purpose of discussing the lives and works of Goethe, Ibsen, Samuel Butler, Chaucer, Shakespeare, and others. "Interest as sustained, as thorough, would be hard to find in any university anywhere," he said.

Talented men in prison are probably not much different from their contemporaries outside, and I must admit we had trouble with some of them. I had one clever reporter whose behavior was beyond reproach when he used a typewriter, but after he was paroled and switched to a fountain pen everything he wrote bounced. Another of our reporters was a dead ringer for actor Lee Tracy, and when he was released two or three years ago he signed checks here and there with Tracy's name. Tracy once visited San Quentin hoping to meet his infamous double, but our former reporter, as they say in the movies, was still on the lam. Still another time, back in 1943, I got a tip that there would be something interesting in a certain February issue of the *News*. I was puzzled about it because I had already seen page proofs of the issue, but decided to check the mail department for papers going to outside subscribers. After unrolling some forty copies, we found one containing two pay-roll checks made out to a Joe Richardson by the Western Pipe & Steel Company, a large San Francisco concern. It took only a few minutes to determine that there was no Joe Richardson and that the checks, though impressive, were forgeries. Two of our inmate printers, it seems, discovered that sample books brought to San Quentin by paper-company salesmen contained sheets of so-called check safety paper. The printers tore out these samples, did the printing in the shop, and managed to get to one of our check-writing machines. They found a confederate outside, arranged to mail the wrapped checks to him at different addresses, and were all set to make a few dollars for themselves. Needless to say, the scheming printers are learning a different trade right now.

We had one other question in connection with the *News* which I don't think we have yet solved properly, and one which may always be debatable because it touches on a much larger and more delicate problem—sex in prison.

In the early issues of the paper we used up a lot of space with what newspapermen call cheesecake—pictures of pretty girls displaying even prettier legs. Later on, during the war, when pin-up girls became standard equipment in the armed forces, we had them in San Quentin too. I can't recall now which one of these charming starlets the inmates voted the one they would most like to be locked up with, but the *News*, like many another paper, printed plenty of these photographs. They were pinned up in cells and carried around in wallets by our men, who had to do their fighting in prison war plants instead of overseas. In 1945 there were complaints that some of the *News* pictures were too risqué, and we were asked to print only those in which the ladies wore adequate clothes. Later an order was issued banning not only pin-up-girl pictures in the cells, but also photographs which showed wives, sweethearts, or other inmate relatives in bathing suits, shorts, or other stages of undress. The order was issued because it was felt that prisoners should not be exposed to tantalizing influences that might, for example, make them restless or want to escape. Personally, I have always thought—and Gladys agrees—that a man who is no longer interested in looking at a pretty girl in a bathing suit might just as well jump off a bridge.

I have heard some penologists say that men doing long terms in prison eventually lose all interest in women. I don't believe that, for in San Quentin I have had more than one demonstration that you cannot lock love and sex out of a man's life. Kid McCoy, for instance, managed to keep a lot of women interested in him, and among others he intrigued a certain countess who kept telephoning me, for some strange reason, long after the Kid was dead. One evening we were at the Curran Theatre in San Francisco, engrossed in an exciting play, when an usher whispered, "Hurry, Warden. There's a break at the prison. They're on the phone about it." I dashed out into the lobby with my blood pressure soaring, wondering why on earth we should have a break after eight quite peaceful years. I picked up the phone and snapped, "This is Duffy."

"Why, hello, Warden," said a sweet, husky voice. "Don't get excited. There isn't any break. This is the countess and I just wanted to talk to you about the Kid and——"

I told the lady what I thought of her, in a blunt but nice way, and she never bothered me again. Dozens of other publicized prisoners, of course, have had mash notes from enamored women they have never met, and sometimes the censors have difficulty cooling off these letters before delivery. Some, in fact, are rejected entirely. There was one letter, however, on which I called off the censors because I knew the men would enjoy it. The letter came from Miss Mae West after two of our artists impulsively composed and illustrated a flowery valentine for her. They sent it to Hollywood and invited her to visit the prison, and she sent this answer:

To the Men of San Quentin:

I want to thank you for your beautiful valentine. It was a lovely thought. And the valentine itself was so artistically lettered and beautifully colored. I imagine you made it there yourselves, as I don't think you could get out to get one. So, because it is your own work, I appreciate it all the more.

Maybe I can return the compliment by "comin' up to see you" in person. Of course I don't think I can improve your minds. I'm afraid that is a little out of my line. But I could try and cheer you up a little. In fact, my gentlemen friends have told me I cheer them up a whole lot. And I guess if I get up there to see you I can at least be a kind of influence, although I can't exactly say what kind. Somehow, I always seem to make a good impression in the worst way.

143

But kidding aside, boys, I would like to see you. It would certainly be a fascinatin' experience to call on so many men—usually they call on me. There must be a lot to learn about San Quentin—but that takes time.

Thanks again for being so nice to me, boys.

Sin-sationally yours,
Mae West

We printed her letter in the *News* with her picture, and copies of that issue are now a collector's item. We were subsequently criticized for giving her the space, on the grounds that the letter was undignified, corny, and probably press-agent-inspired. Even granting the truth of these complaints, I felt that the men genuinely enjoyed the gag, and no amount of jaundice alters the fact that for a week or two they were proud to say to themselves: "Mae West doesn't think she's too good for us . . . she made us feel like men again." There was one other consideration which the public never knew—Mae West was sincerely, not *sin-sationally,* interested in the new San Quentin program, and she sent five hundred dollars to the Inmate Welfare Fund to be spent for whatever the men needed most. And with the check came a short personal note: "No publicity on this, please."

Men in prison who have no women create their own, like Pygmalion. They paint or draw pictures, sometimes nudes, or they fashion female figures from clay, wood, cement, mud, or anything available—all in violation of our rules, of course. I remember one inmate who used to make flowerpots, archways, Greek columns, and other decorative things for the prison gardens. One day, I think I was about fourteen at the time, he took me into his little supply shack and showed me his buried treasure—half a dozen beautiful statues of nude women. I was so scared that I ran out and never mentioned it to anyone, and I don't think he was ever caught. Sometimes we find hidden bathing-girl pictures which have been clipped from the best magazines, when guards make unannounced shakedowns in the never-ending search for contraband. In that connection I concluded some time ago that we might as well entice our art-loving population out into the open, and so I organized the first sketching and painting class the prison ever had. One of our good friends at the nearby College of Marin, the late William Rauschnabel, volunteered to teach the group, and we were able to borrow easels, pencils, and paint. The men would go down on the San Quentin beach, sixteen at a time, to sketch the fishing boats and Paradise Cove across the water, and they subsequently turned in some remarkable work. Some of them, in fact, later obtained work as commercial artists outside. I walked down to the beach to watch them many times, and I couldn't help thinking that in former years any unguarded prisoner standing on that spot might have been smacked with a bullet from one of the tower guns—towers now mostly deserted.

I was first confronted with the whole problem of women in the prison some twenty years ago. At that time there were perhaps one hundred and fifty women prisoners confined in a separate building on the reservation, women who could be seen now and then by the men, and who were only one wall and a fence away from the big cell blocks. Warden Holohan didn't go there often himself, but he sent me to the women's department frequently to hear complaints—such as those from Louise Peete—straighten out feuds, investigate escape plots, or break up "romances" carried on through the medium of smuggled or planted notes. Some of the girls—most of them were actually quite young—showed amazing ingenuity and persistence in keeping those artificial love affairs alive, and many of them would have taken any risk necessary to get their hands on a man. Indeed, I recall one unsuspecting deliveryman from San Rafael who brought a bundle there one day and who was suddenly, but not unwillingly, snatched into a room by two of the girls. There was another incident, when the women's department was still inside the walls, in which a determined male inmate built a trap door connecting one of the women's cells to a clothes locker on his floor, and things were quite cozy for him and the girl until she was paroled. The trap door was not found, by the way, until two other women began scratching each other for the privilege of occupying the vacated cell and inheriting the Lothario from the lower floor. "I'll certainly be relieved," Warden Holohan said one day, "when we can clean out that —— henhouse!" Not long afterward, when the new prison was opened at Tehachapi, Warden Holohan said that at last he could relax.

I remembered all this, of course, when I became warden, and decided to bring groups of carefully selected civilians into the big house. I had always felt it was a mistake to lock men up and throw the key away. I wanted them to believe that they still belonged to the world, that their punishment was not complete exile, but a chance to pay the debt and start over. But throughout the history of

San Quentin most wardens had shown a tendency to shut out the world. Visits were confined to the brief receptions allowed by the rules, very few plain citizens got beyond the main gate, and no women were allowed inside the walls. Consequently many a prisoner going out on parole found the transition a shock. People wore a kind of clothes he hadn't seen for years, they spoke a different language, because he had heard only "main-line" talk, and he was awkward with women because he was not used to having them around.

"But you *can't* bring women inside," one horrified officer said when I told him my plans.

"Why not?"

"With these cons? Why, they'll whistle at 'em, insult 'em, and first thing you know, some guy will make a grab for a girl and you'll have a riot on your hands."

"You can't conceal the fact that half the people in the world are women," I said, "and most of these fellows will be living with women when they get out. I don't think it will hurt them to remember what one looks like. In fact, it might help."

I began bringing mixed groups of visitors into San Quentin late in 1940, and thousands have walked around inside ever since on carefully guided tours. We may have had some fidgety feminine guests over the years, but not one was ever approached, insulted, whistled at, or touched. If anything, the circumspect behavior of our men has been a disappointment to some of the ladies, who admitted they drew wolf calls and whistles almost everywhere else outside. There was some renewed apprehension just a few years ago when we replaced most of the inmate clerks and office workers with women employees, but that revolutionary change started no fires either. The only man really disturbed was Vincent "Pegleg" Lucich, a prohibition-era gunman who was doing a life term and serving as an attendant in the tuberculosis ward of the San Quentin hospital.

"Now, Warden," he said peevishly, "you're puttin' some women nurses in here and it ain't gonna work. These are tough babies I got, and no woman's gonna handle 'em. But they lissen to me."

"Let's give it a try, Vince," I said. "You're probably right—but do the best you can."

A week later Pegleg thumped up to me with a big grin. "Hey, waddaya know, Warden. These nurses are okay. Why, I uster go up to a guy and tell him, 'Take the medicine, you dope,' and they'd gimme a horselaugh. But when these girls come purrin' around, why, they just say, 'Yes, ma'am.'"

And that's how Pegleg was softened and won by the ladies, as, indeed, the other men were. Consider, too, the case of Bill Sansbury, who was saved from another ten-year term just a few months ago because a girl said she had faith in his future. Peggy, whose father is a guard at San Quentin, came to work at the prison in July 1948 and was eventually assigned to the psychiatric department as a clerk. There one of the case histories was young Sansbury, an ex-paratrooper serving his first penitentiary term for burglarizing a store in Los Angeles—a crime for which he confessed there was no reason or justification. Bill made a fine record at San Quentin and was paroled on September 2, 1949, but there was a "hold" against him in Baltimore and he was returned to that city to stand trial on an earlier forgery charge. Three days before Bill left the prison with Baltimore police officers, Peggy resigned her job, withdrew her savings, and left home in a hurry. The next time we heard from her, she popped up in Baltimore just as Bill was being brought into court and begged Judge Robert France to give him another chance. "I know he'll go straight," she said. The sympathetic judge suspended sentence and put Bill on probation for three years. "It is her faith in you," Judge France said, "that is responsible for this suspended sentence."

I admire a woman with trust and courage in her heart, but unhappily there are all too few of them sustaining their men in the blue world of the cell blocks. A woman who will wait for a prisoner while the years crawl by is unusual, and so is one who is not worried by a man's criminal past. As one contrast, for example, I had a phone call not long ago from an excited young man who said: "My girl is here with me, Warden, and we want to get married tonight. But somebody told her I did time in San Quentin and she's upset."

"Did you do time here?"

"No, sir. Never been near the place."

I asked him to put the girl on the line. "Do you love this fellow?" I asked.

"Of course," she said.

"Okay. Will you marry him even if he has a record?"

"Well . . . yes."

I told her to wait while I checked the files, and a few minutes later I confirmed that her young man was telling the truth. She sounded tremendously relieved and gushed her thanks, but I don't think that marriage will go very far.

There are other aspects to the sex-in-prison problem, of course, that are not quite so romantic, but they must be faced. Society cannot ignore the question of homosexuality, neither can a prison warden, and in San Quentin it was a nightmare for years. When I began my first term as warden, the bisexual inmates were still allowed to work and mingle with the other men in the yard, and I knew very well that over the years they had fomented more violence, engaged in more feuds, and perhaps cost more lives than all other prisoners put together. In the old days most of the fights which drew shots from the gun towers had arisen over what are known in prison parlance as "queens," and so naturally I was already convinced that they needed special attention. I was still trying to work out something in April 1941 when an inmate named Reicin disappeared from his workbench in a basement storeroom under the large mess hall. Some of the guards thought Reicin had escaped. But I had a hunch he was dead or wounded somewhere within the walls, because there had been rumors concerning him and two of his homosexual friends, and I heard they had been quarreling. We started search crews through the huge building, and before the day was over, I myself found Reicin's body, with a slashed throat, stuffed into a ventilator in the darkest part of the basement. I got a confession from his murderers, and they were subsequently convicted and transferred to Folsom Prison for life.

We didn't want any more killings that could possibly be avoided, and no time was wasted in doing something about it. We cleaned out the old Spanish cell block, put steel control fences around it, and then rounded up all the known aggressive homosexuals. There were about eighty men altogether, and we put each one into a single cell and assigned them to work in the prison laundry under special guard—the first time in San Quentin history that these unfortunate individuals had been separated from the rest of the men. The first time, you might also say, that they had been given a chance for a fresh start. There have been no bullets whistling at them from gun posts since then, and ninety per cent of our prison sex problems—fights, knifings, thefts, even murder—have been eliminated. You may say, I suppose, that they are still homosexuals, and that segregation is merely a convenient device for getting them out of our hair. You may also believe, as I do, that they are suffering from some sort of personality disorder and that something should be done for them. Something is being done for these men in the psychiatric, religious, and educational departments of the prison right now. Perhaps that will help. But, frankly, I have no prescription for a cure. I hope that men like Dr. Alfred Kinsey will continue their research and come up with some constructive recommendations. Then, if legislators work with specialists in penology, psychiatry, education, religion, and other fields, they will perhaps reach an understanding that will really be helpful.

As a matter of fact, I believe the whole national structure of our law on sex crimes needs serious study. Some are too lenient and some are too strict. No two states are alike in their administration of sex offenses. We have had men doing from twenty to fifty years for "rape" in

San Quentin, for instance—men who would not even have been arrested under similiar circumstances in some other state, as Dr. Kinsey pointed out to us in a recent study here. I know this is not stretching the point, because we had such a case right in the family, you might say. I was in Warden Holohan's office one day going over the file cards of some new prisoners, when I came upon a familiar face. I am not easily flabbergasted, but I was that time, because the prisoner concerned was the former Duffy family physician. Dr. Ramsey, which is not his real name, had known my father long before he came to San Quentin as a guard, and had officiated at the births of my three elder sisters, Ethel, Eva, and Grace. After the third daughter arrived, my father was convinced that Dr. Ramsey was a jinx. "I'm going to get me another doctor," he told my mother, "and maybe he'll deliver us a boy for a change." He actually called in an old Indian medicine man the next two times Mother became pregnant, and on each occasion the tribal wizard handed my father a son. There were two more girls and another boy after that, eight in all—I was the last boy myself—but Dr. Ramsey wasn't given an opportunity for an obstetrical comeback in any of these births, and he soon drifted out of our lives. Now here he was in San Quentin, a broken, tired old man—starting a long jolt for rape, of all things. I went to see him right away, of course, and checked all the facts in the case. Dr. Ramsey, it seemed, had become enamored of a young woman, and for more than a year had provided her with an apartment, a fur coat, and other luxuries. When his practice fell off and he ran out of money, the girl walked out on him and had him arrested for rape. A pious jury convicted the old man in one of the most glaring injustices I have ever known, and he stayed in San Quentin eight long years.

This was not an isolated case, but rather typical of many so-called rape convictions which have brought men to San Quentin with a crushing burden of years. I continue to be confounded and disturbed at some juries that give a man the maximum of fifty years for non-violent intimacies with a willing woman, but will, by contrast, sometimes only slap the wrist of a professional criminal who has stolen their money, jewels, or cars. I have no sympathy, to be sure, for rapists who use force, weapons, drugs, or blackmail, but San Quentin has had some prisoners like Dr. Ramsey who raped by consent, so to speak. There are similar injustices in many other sex cases, such as those which are referred to in the California penal code as "L & L"—or "lewd and lascivious" behavior. It may seem incredible, but we had one man in San Quentin with no previous record who was convicted on this statute because he patted a little girl on the leg while they were seated at a soda fountain. We have had other cases in which the pattern is strikingly similar: A man courts a woman who has a small daughter. Later he decides not to marry the mother, and she, angry or jealous, accuses him of indecently fondling the little girl. Suddenly he is in jail, or on the way to the penitentiary. I followed many of these cases while I was a secretary to the parole board, and I know that in some of them the men were victims of a grave injustice. On the other hand, I strongly believe in long confinement for sex offenders who use force, and for those who molest our children, and if there is need for stronger sex laws, it should be in this field. Dr. Kinsey, whose studies on sexual behavior have aroused so much controversy, recently made a careful analysis of some of our so-called sex criminals at San Quentin. I am not in a position to discuss his findings, but I am hopeful that this sort of research will not only enlighten the scientists but will show the law makers in all our states that it is time for a reappraisal of our outmoded and conflicting codes on sex.

At the present moment, in the opinion of Dr. David Schmidt, San Quentin has about five hundred prisoners who can be termed "psychotic," and there are hundreds more in need of psychiatric treatment. Unfortunately there are only five psychiatrists on the staff at this writing, a pitifully small number to handle the serious problem of the sex offender. Members of the state legislature, as well as other officials, have deplored the increasing number of sex crimes, but when we ask for an increased budget to engage another five psychiatrists, this same legislature turns us down. I sincerely hope that future legislative bodies will grant our Department of Corrections requests for adequate personnel and adequate budgets to care for our wards properly.

Even some of our professional miscreants don't seem to know what it's all about. A prisoner stopped me in the yard one day for something and I asked him why he was in San Quentin.

"It was a sex crime, Warden," he said.

"What do you mean by that?"

"I gave a woman a black silk nightgown."

"But that's not a sex crime," I said.

"Yes, it was," he insisted. "After I gave it to her she ran out on me and went with some other guy. When I asked her for the nightgown back, she wouldn't give it to me."

"But I still don't see——"

"Well, Warden," he said, "that's when I bumped her off."

6

The kid in solitary was doing his time hard.

He was in the shadows at the dark end of the cell, flattened against the wall like a bat, and even in the half-light I could see the snarl on his face.

"Bill," I said, "I want to talk to you."

"Leave me alone," he said.

I glanced down at the file card in my hand and read it again. Yates, William. Age, 19. White. Native of Nevada. Robbery, 1st degree, five counts. Five to life on each. The boy was good-looking, even in the harsh prison mug pasted on the card. Dark eyes, curly black hair, high cheekbones, and a strong chin. Too much chin, evidently, because he had been sticking it out ever since he came to San Quentin, and the record was discouraging: "Cursed the guards, slugged another inmate, caught gambling, refused to work." Even in solitary he had flooded his cell, torn up a mattress, and thrown food through the bars.

"Why don't you take it easy, Bill?" I said. "What's the trouble?"

"Take it easy?" He bounded out of the corner, suddenly tense and alive. "Take it easy when they keep ridin' me? They're tryin' to break me, see. I wasn't doin' a damn thing this time except foolin' around with my toothbrush."

"What were you doing with the toothbrush?"

"I was moldin' the handle. I found out I could soften it up and bend it. A guy's gotta do somethin'."

"The lieutenant probably figured you were making a shiv."

"Listen, Warden," he said brusquely, "I'm no pig-sticker. If I wanna cut up a guy, I can do it better with my hands."

"Well, what were you making?"

"A ring, Warden. Nuthin' else. For that they gimme five days up here in the hole, and they squawk because I blow my top. It ain't fair."

"Okay, Bill," I said. "I'll look into it and talk to you tomorrow."

A little later that afternoon, as I walked across the big yard and saw thousands of men floating aimlessly over the concrete sea, I felt a little guilty about fellows like Bill Yates. They simply didn't have enough to do. Time in prison is tenacious and hard to kill, and in the San Quentin of 1940 there was too much time left after the state had claimed its eight hours a day from a man. Time in the cell blocks, from late afternoon until the next morning. Time in the yard on week ends, when for most men there was nothing to do except brood or plot. Ironically, even if a man wanted to make something with his hands in his spare time, he could not use San Quentin tools or materials, and if he was ingenious enough to beat that handicap, he risked the solitary cells and loss of credits. I wasn't quite sure what to do about it, but at least I could make a start.

The next morning I drove to San Francisco, made the rounds of my friends in the big downtown hotels, and collected a whole shoebox full of discarded toothbrushes, most of which had colored handles. I found a pamphlet on plastics in a secondhand bookstore, and I bought some acetone, a few little tools, and some other harmless chemicals. I wrapped up the whole kit and took it to Bill's solitary cell in the north block.

"Here you are, son," I said. "If you want to play with toothbrushes, see what you can do with these. I'll issue a permit so the officers won't bother you."

A week later, after he had gone back to his own cell, I saw Bill in the yard. "I've been lookin' for you, Warden," he said. He fumbled in his pockets, brought out a fistful of beautiful plastic rings, and poured them into my cupped hands. "They ain't very good yet," he said self-consciously, "but I thought you might like to have them." During the next six months Bill stayed out of trouble and fashioned hundreds of those colored rings. At his insistence, I always filled my pockets with them whenever I went out to make a talk about the prison, and gave them away as San Quentin souvenirs. Later on, after he had perfected the process, Bill began taking orders not only for the rings but for brooches, earrings, and other ornaments. During the war he worked night and day without any pay, filling orders for servicemen who wanted his plastic jewelry for trading in the South Pacific, but when he was finally paroled he had saved some two thousand dollars from sales to civilians. He used the money to start a small plastics business on the West Coast, and in his spare time he taught his art to wounded soldiers in army hospitals. I am sure that Bill Yates will never do time again.

There were other men like Yates, of course. In every prison from seven to ten per cent of the prisoners are malcontents, incorrigibles, and troublemakers who, as any warden knows, are not all likely to respond to a helping hand. I was under no illusions about San Quentin's bad boys, and I doubted whether very many of them would react to the toothbrush approach. But neither was I willing to bring back strait jackets and the rubber hose, though a few of the older officers kept warning me that this nursery-school system, as some called it, would bring on a bloody mess someday. Indeed, at one convention of prison administrators one of my fellow wardens spoke out quite frankly along the same line. "I don't go for sob-sister stuff," he said. "We're getting too damn soft. Out at our place we use a strap with good psychological effect. The men fear it and behave accordingly." Not long afterward, unfortunately, the psychological effect backfired in that institution, and there was a terrible riot during which several lives were lost.

I didn't want any riots in San Quentin, naturally, and I was convinced there would not be any if I could keep all the men so busy with work, education, religion, hobbies, entertainment, and sports that they would not have time to plot. I called on a legislator friend of mine and asked him to write a bill that would permit prisoners to make things on their own time and at their own expense, and sell them at San Quentin.

"You must be out of your head, Clint," he said. "The labor lobby will make hash out of you, and the manufacturers will scream about competition from convicts."

"Yes," I said, "and while they're doing it they will also yell about the high cost of crime and prisons. Anyway, my boys won't be out in the open market. The bill must stipulate that all sales are to be made at the prison, and you know the public won't be stampeding San Quentin for any Monday morning bargain sales."

"All right," he said.

"Fine," I said. "You write the bill and I'll lobby it myself."

I went to Sacramento with my bill, which was actually only a hundred words long, and talked to every legislator who would listen. I was in smoke-filled rooms, and I knocked on sacred doors, and before long they were calling the measure "Duffy's Folly." But to my pleasant surprise it sailed through without much opposition, and was signed into law by the governor on May 28, 1941. The very next day, wasting no time, we formed the San Quentin Hobby Association. We had no textbooks, tools, teachers, or a place to work, but by scrambling around we solved those problems in a week. I borrowed some books from the libraries and bought a few others. Some of the men bought tools with their meager savings, and we got the rest on loan from the jute mill and other shops. We tore out a partition in an old building to make a shop, and I assigned Guard William Pelleschi to the hobby-work program. Later we had some teachers from the Marin County schools assigned as hobby instructors.

The first products that emerged from this unusual factory were pretty crude and were hardly worth giving away. But with the help of such good San Quentin friends as the late Alfred Light of Philadelphia, Mrs. A. D. Bishop of Orange, California, R. E. Trickle of the *Wall Street Journal*, and others, the men were able to buy better equipment. Mr. Light, whose recent death was a great loss to his friends in San Quentin, came to the prison many times to watch his protégés at work, and one of his last gifts was a substantial sum of money for the establishment of a loan fund for the hobby program. He named it the Eugenia Duffy Memorial Fund, in memory of my mother, and the money was made available to talented inmates who could not buy their own tools or materials. In time, as the work improved, the customers began to respond, and today more than one thousand San Quentin inmates work on the hobby program at night, making fine belts, wallets, picture frames, jewelry, greeting cards, toys, and other goods. The men found a particular delight in the fact that among their best customers were policemen, deputy sheriffs, and detectives, who paid fancy prices for hand-tooled gun holsters made by the men they sent to prison. The whole business expanded so rapidly that we had to block off a section of the reception room and open a retail store which, during visiting hours, is lined with customers from a dozen different states. The hobby shop has won state-fair prizes, and once took a second prize in the National Window Display contest. It's a nice, smart little shop, run by the inmates under the guidance of our educational supervisor, Alfred G. Rowan, and many a visiting department-store man has offered to buy our entire stock, which of course is not possible under the law.

Not so long ago one of these merchants, examining the stack of costly items in the showcase, looked suspiciously at the dexterous young inmates working behind the counter.

"Say," he whispered, "doesn't anybody ever steal any of this stuff?"

"Of course," I said.

"I thought so," he said righteously.

"Yes," I added, "we've had things stolen right off the counters—by visitors."

During the early stages of this program I was approached in the yard one day by a middle-aged man—let's call him Doc Porter—who hadn't shown much interest in anything at San Quentin.

"Warden," he said, "can anybody get into this hobby-shop deal?"

"Certainly," I said. "What do you want to do?"

"Well . . ." He looked at me hesitantly. "I got some ideas, but I haven't a dime to my name. Do you suppose I could go on the cuff for a big block of soft wood?"

I told him I would try. A day or two later I drove into San Rafael and picked up a huge chunk of soft pine for about seven-fifty and gave it to Doc. Some weeks later, when I had forgotten the incident, Doc walked into the office on a special pass and presented me with an exquisitely carved bas-relief of Will Rogers astride his favorite horse.

"Where'd you learn to do that, Doc?" I asked.

"That's nothin', Warden," he said, a little abashed. "When I was a kid in Tennessee everybody was carvin' wood like crazy, and I guess I went along with 'em."

But Doc didn't stop with his gift to me. He whittled out salad servers, plates, ash trays, statuettes, and dozens of other articles, and sold them all in the hobby shop for a net profit of about fifteen hundred dollars in four years. Once, during the war, he carved a statue and donated it for a war-bond sale in San Francisco. The statue was auctioned off for one hundred and fifty thousand dollars' worth of bonds, and Doc broke down and wept when I told him the news. He has been out on parole for several years now, earning a decent living with his talented hands, and proud that he has also won the respect of his neighbors.

Another whose gallant spirit I admired was a gaunt, taciturn artist I will call Ray Richards, who came to San Quentin in 1933 with two life sentences for a first-degree murder conviction in Los Angeles. Ray was one of those ordinary, law-abiding citizens who suddenly became involved in a violent family quarrel during which he shot and killed his wife and his sister-in-law. He was lucky to escape the gallows—he told me many times that he deserved to be hanged—and when he came to prison he felt he was through with life. The first two or three years, like most lifers, Ray floundered in an abyss of despair and inertia and showed little or no interest in painting or cartooning. One day, according to his own version, Ray was working as an attendant in the prison hospital and caring for a dying prisoner. The ward was dark and depressing; there was neither light nor beauty on the blank walls, and it struck him as the loneliest place on earth. He asked if he could have brushes and color, and he began to paint on the vacant walls. As the months and years moved on, Ray Richards went from room to room in the hospital, the library, the reception room, and other buildings—every place where the walls were cold and gray—and painted magnificent murals. He did landscapes, biblical tableaux, trains, planes, famous buildings, and historical scenes. He worked fifteen hours a day for more than eight years—and he knew that all of his works, more than one hundred murals, would be lost to him forever because they were painted directly on the walls. And when the hobby program began, he turned out hundreds of cartoons, greeting cards, table decorations, book covers. In 1943, when the legislature permitted deserving prisoners to enlist in the armed forces through a special San Quentin selective-service board, a group of army officers came over one day looking for men qualified for camouflage training. I escorted them around the reservation and pointed out the paintings on the walls.

"It's wonderful work," one officer said. "How big is your staff of artists?"

"I don't have a staff," I said. "All these paintings were done by one man who wanted to put some beauty into the place. It's his way of paying for what he did."

"We need men with that kind of guts," the officer said. "We'll take him."

Ray was paroled to the army, at the age of fifty-two, and his brushes went to war. He performed with distinction, and our files were soon filled with letters from his commanding officers praising his work, his loyalty, and the respect he had earned from men of every rank. He is free now, and successfully established in business, but he will never be forgotten in San Quentin, where his art wiped out much of the drabness and gloom.

The amount of money earned by our artisans behind walls, though small, is impressive, and many a struggling family has been held together or kept off the relief rolls with funds the men send home. But more important is the fact that hundreds of men have learned a trade, a business, or a profitable hobby, and they have left San Quentin with money in their pockets and courage for the future, instead of just a new suit and a token payment from the state. Here's a man who had a psychic limp when he came to prison, and had no interest in anything. Now he's a craftsman in a novelty factory, making miniature covered wagons he first developed at San Quentin. Here is a middle-aged Negro who had served two prior terms for robbery and could barely write his own name. He went to school in San Quentin, revealed a surprising talent for art, and began making hand-lettered greeting cards which have already earned him a substantial sum. We have men making and selling jewelry, hand-woven scarves, model planes, toy animals, inlaid-wood articles, and other items —men who had wasted their lives in petty thefts and crude forgeries and who were always just one jump ahead of the police. There are literally hundreds of others who have taken their hobby-shop training into outside factories and shops and are earning weekly salaries they never thought possible.

Some of the boys, I confess, couldn't get all the larceny out of their hearts and worked overtime on schemes to pick up a dishonest dollar. We had one young man with a rare talent for lettering and scrollwork who decided to make diplomas, medical degrees, and similar documents as a side line. He turned out some beautiful Baptist ministerial certificates and was doing very well selling them until we rudely took away his pens and brushes. There was another man whose secret hobby was the manufacture of playing cards, which are contraband in San Quentin, but he furnished his own punishment, you might say, because every time he sold a new deck he got into a secret poker game and was promptly cleaned. Inevitably, there were also a few inmates whose inventive ability was applied to new escape techniques. Inmate Tiblow, for instance, constructed a very lifelike dummy and left it in his cell while he climbed to the jute-mill roof on his way out. He was exposed by a big spotlight and ignominiously hauled down, but he did contribute something, though, because ever since we have made all inmates stand at the cell doors for the evening count, and none of them has yet invented a dummy that can walk and talk. Inmate Roncelli, who was mechanically minded, also endowed us with a new idea by hiding himself under the altered hood of an outgoing automobile. He didn't stay out very long, and nowadays, just in case someone else has discovered how to do it, we search the engine compartments of all departing cars, as well as the trunk space in the rear.

One of our most disappointing failures was a notorious killer, Albert Tinnin, who came to San Quentin with Frank Egan, the former public defender of San Francisco. Egan and Tinnin, along with a bumbling individual named Verne Doran, were convicted of murdering an elderly woman for her insurance in a case that shocked complacent San Francisco. Egan was a stunned and bitter man when he first came to prison, but soon rallied and began devoting his time to the San Quentin library, the inmate council, and other activities. But Tinnin remained frosty and aloof for a long time, finally taking an interest in the

166

creation of hand-tooled leather wallets. He became so adept at the art that his products outsold those of other craftsmen three to one. Unfortunately, though he was sending home a few dollars now and then, he had the soul of a racketeer and began doing a brisk side-line trade in smuggled benzedrine. We finally caught him with a supply of the drug and broke up his clique and transferred him in a hurry to Folsom Prison. But for every man who is a "wrong guy," as the inmates might put it, there are a hundred others who have kept faith with us and their fellow workers on the hobby plan and who are, or will be, making good in the free world outside.

During the early stages of this program I had a note from one of the prison jesters saying that his favorite hobby was going to the movies but he didn't see how he could pursue it at San Quentin. We joked about it once in a while in the yard, but he didn't know I had already considered the subject. It was not a matter of pampering the men, or establishing just another prison precedent; it was just one more way of keeping them in touch with their lost world outside the walls, a world that needed to be kept attractive so they would work to regain their place in it. There were some practical aspects, too, such as improving our educational system through the use of training films. But it was virtually a hopeless idea, because the state could not finance it, and projectors, films, and equipment were too expensive even for the inmate fund. Later, during the spring of 1941, I was in Los Angeles on business and dropped in to see an old friend, Harry Warner.

"Tell me, Clint," he said during the course of the conversation, "how do the men at San Quentin like the new pictures we're turning out?"

"We don't have them in San Quentin," I said.

"What?" he said in a wounded tone. "No movies at all?"

"Not even a newsreel. In fact, we have some men who haven't been in a theater since the old silent-film days."

I suppose it was inconceivable to Mr. Warner that there could be anywhere in the world an audience of five thousand men that had somehow eluded Warner Bros. He was so disturbed, I am glad to say, that he scurried around the studio and found two old projectors, which he promptly shipped to San Quentin with a dozen cans of film. I located a couple of projectionists who were temporarily retired in the south cell block, and a master mechanic, and together they started repairing the machines. I had misgivings about this undertaking, to be sure, because I had not forgotten Warden Holohan's biting response some years earlier when I had broached the subject while I was his secretary. "Now, Clinton," he said, "you know that's a damn-fool idea. Can't you imagine what would happen the minute you put several thousand men into an auditorium and turn out the lights? Why, every sorehead in the place would take care of his beefs in the dark, and you wouldn't have room for all the bodies." I knew he was exaggerating in order to make his point, but I conceded that perhaps there were some risks involved. Nevertheless, now that I was ready, I wouldn't back down, and I was confident the men would behave.

On a Sunday afternoon in July 1941, San Quentin's mess hall was jammed with every man who could make the show. The lights went down, a few guards shifted uneasily, and machinery whirred in the makeshift projection room to start the first talking motion picture ever shown behind our walls. I sat there in the darkness, listening for any unusual sounds that might mean trouble among the men. But there was nothing. I was conscious of the scratchy loudspeaker and the sputtering of our imperfect projection lamps, but no one else heard this distracting noise. For these men were free again, if only for an hour; the steel and stone melted away, and the magic of the sound screen gave a lift to their hearts. I am sure that no audience anywhere ever cursed the villain with more gusto or laughed louder at a hoary joke, and when the picture faded out the applause was frightening. I was standing at the door when the men filed out to return to their cells, and I saw more than one furtively wiping his eyes and trying to look tougher than he ever looked before. And in the hall there were a few of the older men, still hunched in their front-row seats, sobbing and telling the guards to go away and leave them alone. I heard them say there was no law to make them do their time hard, and that they would never come to a show again—but they did.

Thanks to our Hollywood friends who lend us the films, we have had movies in San Quentin ever since, and in all those years there has not been a single incident to give me any regrets. The men have kept up with the world, its fashions and fads, its politics and preachings—and that has probably been good for them all. The weekly shows are a privilege, not a right, and only those with good conduct and work records are allowed to go. I think I can say that today most of our men would rather be punished with the old-fashioned strap than lose their pass for the movie hall on week ends.

With motion pictures showing regularly in the prison, it was inevitable that some of the inmates would become rabid movie fans and start writing letters to their favorite players. I have never known an actor or actress who did not send back a gracious acknowledgment, and before long many of the Hollywood people were making personal appearances at San Quentin. Most of these visits were and are impromptu, and without the usual fanfare of publicity, and consequently mean much more to the men. Leo Carrillo has dropped in many times, for instance, and never fails to get a roar from the men, especially the Mexican inmates, when he says: "'Allo, I come to see all my Spanish cousins." Joe E. Brown, William Powell, Walter Slezak, Glenn Ford, Edward G. Robinson, Caesar Romero—among others—have taken the prison tour and left the inmates goggle-eyed. Otto Kruger went through our identification bureau one day and made friends at once by posing for a "mug" picture with a plaque around his neck which, instead of the usual number, read: "Otto Kruger—Convicted of Being a Great Actor. Not a Felony in California."

Another time Artie Shaw brought his orchestra over to play in the mess hall, and the jam session that followed rattled every window on the reservation. I have been told that motorists two miles from the prison heard the bellow of voices and stepped on the gas to get out of the danger zone. Artie later came down from the stage, dripping perspiration, and said to his manager: "Tell my booker I don't want to play any more theaters or hotels. Tell him just to book me into prisons."

To an outsider, I suppose, these incidents would seem trivial and irrelevant. But in San Quentin any little thing that turns the mind from normal routine is a shaft of light in a shadowy world—the honking of geese winging southward, a fisherman's dory knifing the whitecaps below the parapets, a pretty girl flying down the walk to catch the San Rafael bus, or the San Quentin kids trudging homeward from school and kicking invisible pebbles with their toes. Only in prison, for instance, would you find a man who befriended a two-legged mouse and built a tiny ramp on which it could reach a nest above his bunk. One day the mouse ventured outside the cell block and there, alas, was gobbled up by a cat. The prisoners' search for companionship has made pets of sea gulls, turtles, rats, and cockroaches, and once two men were nearly murdered because they captured and cooked another inmate's tame duck. It is not surprising, then—to go to the other extreme—that men and women who are important names in the entertainment world bring something intangible but wonderful into a place like San Quentin—a fraternization which, if it lasts only half an hour, makes exile easier to bear. Only men in prison could say, as one group did when I started to introduce them to Lippy Durocher and his pretty wife, Laraine Day: "Yes, sir, Warden—we spotted Lippy and Miss Day when they was comin' through the gate." The gate was two hundred and fifty yards away. Lippy was so pleased with this tribute that he slipped on a baseball uniform, bounced around the field with the prison team for an hour, and subsequently sent us a dozen big-league bats and balls.

Not long after we started the movie program I realized that, except for the tubercular patients in the hospital, the condemned men were the only prisoners unable to see the shows, though they, of all men, needed forgetfulness the most. There was a time, under previous wardens, when the condemned men were allowed to watch baseball games. But it was a nerve-jangling security problem that called for extra guards, complete separation from other prisoners, and constant surveillance of each man. Even then there were dangerous crises, such as the time an appointed gang killer blew a poisoned arrow at a lifer who had been assigned to Row duties for his own safety. The shaft pierced his neck as he sat on the special bench with the condemned, and only prompt medical attention saved his life.

Obviously I could not bring the doomed prisoners into the mess hall, but I didn't see anything wrong with showing pictures right on the Row. One April morning in 1943, when I finally got some long-delayed equipment, I made up my mind to try it. I took a portable projector, a screen, and a 16-mm. feature production and carried them in the elevator to the top floor of the north cell block. I went through the double gates into the long corridor of Condemned Row, where some thirteen men were out of their cells for the recreation period, and put the projector on a table.

"Fellows," I said, "we're going to have some movies."

The men suddenly froze where they stood, and in the silence the gun guard's shoes sounded like sandpaper as he took out his pistol and edged along the wire cage that separated him from the Row. It was a tense moment for me, which I tried to conceal, and the Row guards admitted

172

later they couldn't have been more stunned if one of the prisoners had popped up with a tommy gun. No warden had ever stepped into that steel coop without guards when all the condemned prisoners were loose, but I counted on that fact and hoped I had not misjudged any of those thirteen men. I didn't give them much time to think it over, and it only took a moment to close the blackout windows—this was during the war—and turn out the lights. The picture was soon flickering on the screen, and I sat among them with the feeling that it was I, not they, who had been granted a very special favor. I knew them all. I knew that sooner or later I would have to put them to death, one by one, and I wondered if they understood that it would not be my hand giving the order, but the official hand of Warden Duffy, as required by law.

I looked around in the dim smoky light from the projector, and I could make out some of the faces. There was Glenard Brown, a young sheepherder from the mountains, who had bludgeoned an old woman for her money. Next to him sat Wilson de la Roi, the harelipped Folsom killer who never had much chance as a kid and who would soon die after eleven torturing reprieves. There was Ivan Baa, a slim young Negro who shot a Chinese gambler; and Florencio Alcalde, a Spanish boy who killed his sweetheart. And up in front was Warren Cramer, who disturbed me most of all. He was a slight, wide-eyed, and handsome young man about twenty-five years old, with a deceptive charm and a brilliant analytical mind. But I rarely thought of him as a man, because to me he was still a curly-haired little youngster I had known in the San Quentin village more than fifteen years before. He used to come to the prison with his father, who was related to one of our guards, and everyone knew him as a pleasant, happy boy who enjoyed playing with the other lads in Prison Town. I lost track of Warren for a number of years, but one March day in 1937 he came back—shocking us all—with handcuffs on his wrists and a record as a stick-up man. I got him a job in the parole board offices, where I was then a secretary, and we had many long and—I thought—helpful talks about prisons and crime. He had a flawless record during his five years in San Quentin, and we were all proud of him when he was paroled in 1942. On July fifth, three months after he left prison, Warren walked into a San Francisco drugstore and poked a gun at the clerk, Ernest Sexton.

"Get your hands up," said Warren, "or I'll kill you!"

Unfortunately for them both, Sexton was a fatalist. "We all have to get it sooner or later," he said, coming out from behind the counter, "and if you get me now, you'll get yours later when you're caught." Warren fired one fatal shot point-blank, pocketed the gun, and walked out. He was picked up by the police within twenty-four hours, quickly tried and sentenced to death. He announced in open court that he would not file an appeal and would resist any attempts to investigate the case or delay the execution. I was sick about the case, of course—not so much because Warren Cramer was going to die—he had asked for it —but because I felt we had all failed somewhere along the line. I went up to Condemned Row the day he was brought in, remembering a little note he had written to Gladys two years before. "The warden needs your support, Mrs. Duffy," he had said, "because he will no doubt pass through some rather dark and trying experiences during

174

his tenure of office." I don't think I could have had a more dark and trying experience than this. I was baffled. I felt defeated.

"Why . . . why did you do this, Warren?" I asked.

"I don't know, sir," he said, looking straight at me through the bars. "I just don't know."

"Don't you realize where you are? Don't you know what *this* cell means?"

"Yes, I know. I'm going to die. But please don't worry about me. It has to be done, Warden. I know that if I went out I would kill again, and maybe again. Something makes me—well, it's better this way."

He begged me not to attempt any analysis of his crimes and he wanted nothing done for him. But on this April morning, with only thirty-five days to live, he was plainly enjoying the movies, and he was the first to applaud when the two-hour show came to an end. He came up to me with a smile after the lights were on and reached for my hand.

"You will probably never know just what you achieved here today," he said. "These fellows could have killed you, Warden. Or they could have grabbed you and used you some way. They've talked about that, and they've talked about escape. That's how it is up here—and you know it. But today you did something for us all. You took a hell of a chance—and you won."

On May fifteenth, with more unaffected calm and dignity than I have ever seen in the death house, Warren Cramer sat down in the metal chair to die. He bowed politely to the witnesses, and as the white tendrils of gas spiraled up around his face he turned toward the window and smiled. "Here it comes, Warden . . . so long."

There is one other ancedote I have never told about this boy's distorted but brilliant mind. One afternoon a month or two before Cramer was executed one of our staff psychologists went up to the Row to give I.Q. tests to a group of new arrivals, one of whom was Glenard Brown, the California hillbilly. When Brown's paper was graded, he was given an I.Q. of 147, which is close to the genius level, and for a while he was an object of wonder. But when the doctors returned to extract more pearls of intellect from the youthful marvel, Brown turned out to be quite dull and couldn't answer the simplest questions. Eventually we discovered that the psychologist had left the Row for a while during the examination and that Cramer, in a spirit of whimsey, had answered all the questions for Brown. So it was Cramer whose I.Q. was really 147, but no one ever came around to probe his mind.

We have shown motion pictures on Condemned Row once a week for almost six years now, and sometimes I sit with the men. But I am a little more prudent about it today, because one of those planned visits nearly cost me my life. It began with a rumor in January 1945 that some man on the Row had threatened to crash out. We had no definite information, but as a precaution I stationed extra gun guards outside the long wire cage. Weeks passed, but nothing happened, and I went ahead with plans to attend church services on the Row on Washington's Birthday. At that time there were a number of unreliable men awaiting execution—professional thugs and killers who knew they were washed up and consequently would have nothing to lose in a break. Among them were Djory Nagle, an Oakland robber who had kidnaped and wantonly murdered a taxi driver with the help of two female crooks; Silas Kelso, who had killed a Los Angeles theater owner during a holdup; and Alfred Cavazos, who had made his living with guns. All of them had lost their appeals, and Cavazos had only twenty-four hours of life left. Shortly before noon on February twenty-second, while Father George O'Meara and Chaplain Harry Warwick were conducting their respective services in the long corridor outside the cells, these three men began fidgeting in their seats and glancing expectantly toward the gate. I know now that they were waiting for me. My luck must have been with me that day. I was on my way to the Row when an officer interrupted me outside the cell block and said I was needed at the recreation area where the holiday boxing matches were under way. Some ten minutes later, when the services were over and Nagle saw that I wasn't coming to the Row in time, he nudged Kelso and Cavazos and crooked his finger toward the gate. The three prisoners sidled down the hall just as Chaplain Warwick and Officer W. A. Patterson were wheeling out the small portable organ they had used for the morning hymns. As Patterson opened the gate they knocked him flat, broke his ankle, and stabbed him half a dozen times with stilettos made from bedsprings. They ran for the narrow exit, but it was already too late. The gate was slammed shut, and the gun guard around the corner opened up with his .38. Cavazos was knocked over with a bullet that tore through his hip, and the other two hastily threw down their daggers and quit. By the time I reached the Row everything was under control. Cavazos died in the prison hospital that night, and Nagle and Kelso even-

tually went to the chair. The plot, as it was pieced together, was quite simple. They had planned to use me as a
shield in their rush through the gate, thinking that the
guards wouldn't shoot at such close range if I were in line
of fire. The scheme went awry when I did not come, and
since they were reluctant to seize either of the chaplains,
they vented their fury on the guard. None of the three
plotters knew, I believe, that they would have failed anyway. I instructed all guards long ago to shoot any man who
kidnaps me in an escape attempt, even though I might get
hit myself, and that order still holds. It is the only safe way
you can run a prison where a handful of dangerous men
may use force to make a break for it. The inmate who
wishes to do his time the right way wants and appreciates
rules like this. They are for his protection too.

During the early months of my wardenship, when
there were so many of these new activities under way,
such as the movies and the hobby shop, my office was
swamped with suggestions the men thought I might like.
Some of these inmate ideas were pretty silly, others were
quite good. In either case I was glad to have the men take
an active interest in the rebuilding of their town. I wanted
them to have a voice in the program too, and with that in
mind I organized what was probably the first prison "house
of representatives" anywhere in the world. In the old days
"con bosses" just about ruled San Quentin—with front
office approval—by virtue of their underworld standing,
their toughness, or their intimate knowledge of the prison
and its ways. It was a vicious and demoralizing system,
rotten with favoritism and graft, and no one will ever know
how many prisoners were wounded or killed because they

tried to resist it. The new organization, called the Inmate Departmental Representative Committee—IDRC for short —has functioned without interruption for more than eight years, and in many ways it is the heart of the inmate body. The men on this council represent every section of the prison, are elected by secret ballot, and choose their own chairman.

It is truly the democratic process in action at the big house, because when they meet on Sunday nights they are men once again, freely debating the problems of five thousand other men who cannot always speak for themselves. No officials or guards come into the hall when the council meets; I do not go there myself unless I am asked. Occasionally there are invited guests—officers and civilian employees—who discuss departmental problems with the council. There is a deep sense of pride in the committee's work, with such an *esprit de corps* that more than one elected representative has withdrawn because he felt unworthy of the honor.

It would be embarrassing to you and the council [one man wrote] to find a man with my police record in that group. Also, I could never muster the courage to act as an usher at your public gatherings, as some IDRC men do. The lines of a misspent life are so deeply engraved on my face that my appearance before any civilian is bound to leave a false impression.

It is through these IDRC meetings that we can often feel the real pulse of San Quentin—the beefs, the quarrels, the big and little heartaches, the trivial gripes that loom so large behind walls. They talk about the soup that wasn't so good the other day, or the refuse piling up in the yard. They kick about the laundry work when it's bad, the dust in the mill, or the need for more air in the cell blocks at night. Someone's not getting the San Quentin *News,* or the plumbing has gone wrong in the baths. These things are all typed into the minutes that come to my desk, and decisions are made for the greater good of all.

Sometimes, when I am invited to the IDRC meetings, the council members and I jointly work out a new idea. San Quentin's first Canteen, for instance, evolved from one of these talks, and it has done more for the men than most of the penalties and preaching combined. We who are free take our little luxuries for granted—cigarettes, candy bars, cookies, fruit juice, postage stamps, even toothpaste and soap. There was a time in San Quentin's dark years when a man could be whipped or thrown into the dungeons for having any of these things. When I was a boy with my paper route inside the prison, the prisoners would beg me for a piece of chocolate, and I gave it to them on occasion. One of them was Charley Sharkey, a highway bandit who was going out soon, and every time I saw him he showed me a calendar on which he had checked off each passing day. I think my father suspected what I was doing, but because he was a prison guard with an understanding heart, he never brought it up. Still later, when I was with Warden Holohan, I saw the fabulous traffic in these contraband goods and knew of men who risked all sorts of punishment to get candy, tailor-made cigarettes, or even a little sugar to cook up in some secret place. Men were still gambling for these luxuries when I became warden, and an extra sack of tobacco, for example, was as good as money on the prison exchange.

We opened the Canteen in August 1941, and that was the end of the black market in most forbidden things. Today any inmate in good standing can use his own money, by means of a Canteen card, to buy the articles for which he would have gambled, fought, or suffered pain not many years ago. The profits of the Canteen go into the Inmate Welfare Fund, and that in turn brings other things that help a man fight his battle for redemption—sports, books, music, religion, and the chance to go to school while he's doing his time.

Incidentally, I solved most of the tobacco gambling problem too. I didn't see any reason for limiting the amount of roll-your-own a man could have, because we were processing plenty of it in our plant, and one day I decided to make an experiment. I had the carpenters make a lot of dispenser boxes and had them hung on the walls all over the prison with signs that read: "Help Yourself. No Limit." The tobacco plant superintendent was aghast, anticipating a stampede that would exhaust his supplies, and some of the guards thought I ought to have my head examined. Sixty days later, when we went over the books, tobacco consumption had dropped thirty per cent to an all-time low. This was explained by the fact that when there was a three-sack limit per week even non-smokers were taking all they could get because the tobacco could be used for gambling. The steady gamblers were also hoarding large quantities of it. But with plenty of tobacco available, the men took only what they needed, the gamblers were stuck with their hidden hoards, and consumption was sharply cut. San Quentin's men may still be gambling secretly on this or that, but they're not using our prison tobacco for money because, I can say cheerfully, it isn't worth a darn any more.

The inmates, incidentally, have an affection for their prison-made tobacco, and many use it in preference to standard-brand cigarettes, even though they can afford to buy them. There are even some paroled men who, clinging to habit and the deceptive element of nostalgia, have tried to buy some of the tobacco. It is not for sale, of course, and cannot be obtained outside of California prisons and jails, but I doubt very much whether any ex-inmate would really enjoy the memories stirred by the flavor or fragrance of our product. Incidentally, we call our tobacco "Topper of Quentin," a name that has a curious background. Some years ago I bought a black cocker spaniel for Gladys as a Christmas present.

"What's his name?" she asked.

"I don't know," I said. "Let's have a contest and ask the inmates for suggestions."

I offered a ten-dollar prize, and at the time it seemed as if every man in San Quentin had submitted an entry. We were deluged with letters of every shape, size, and color, and some men sent in long lists. Toward the end of the week, when we had seen everything from Aaron to Zedekiah, we came upon the following letter from Doc Porter, the talented wood carver:

Dear Warden:

After seeing Mrs. Duffy's pup New Year's Day, I think he is Tops, and from the applause he got from the boys they think so too. Just call him Topper, or Tops for short.

That ended the contest. Doc Porter won the prize, and the dog was subsequently registered in the American Kennel Club as "Topper of Quentin." Later on, when we had a contest to name our tobacco, another inmate knew a good thing when he heard it and said: "The dog is Tops. So is the local weed. Call it 'Topper' too." And Topper it was, and is, although some newly arrived inmates, sampling the tobacco and learning how it was named, have said ungratefully that whoever processed the tobacco must have ground up the dog in it too.

7

One Sunday afternoon many years ago the late Harry Houdini amazed several thousand San Quentin prisoners with a demonstration of his remarkable talent for escaping from handcuffs, chains, and other restraining devices. After the performance, which the inmates viewed with what you might call a keen professional interest, my father met a gray-haired lifer who had been around San Quentin for years.

"Well, Ed," my father said, "that Houdini put on a great show, didn't he?"

"That he did, Mr. Duffy," the prisoner replied. "But just the same," he added, with his eyes sparkling in unshakable home-town pride, "I bet some of our boys could show him a trick or two."

I remember that story every time a man tries to escape from San Quentin, and sometimes I think the old lifer understated the case. I can still see simple Ad Arkeley, for instance, calmly swimming away from the prison and waving foolishly to us every time we ordered him to come ashore. We finally had to chase him in a motorboat. I recall when Ernest Booth, the famous prison author, failed in one of his many spectacular escapes. He swung out of a window in the San Quentin hospital and smashed both his legs on the pavement because another prisoner cut the rope to which he clung. I think of Pruzynski, who had himself shipped out of San Quentin in a furniture crate; Martin, who hid in an incinerator and could have been roasted alive; Davis, who lowered himself into a milk truck tank and paddled around in it until the vehicle passed a road block; Marcias and Wells, who hurled Molotov cocktails at a guard tower and escaped in the fiery confusion that followed; Edison, who stole women's clothing from a guard's home and minced out the main gate after soft-soaping a rookie guard.

I don't think there are many prisoners who, at one time or another, have not considered their chances for escape. Perhaps the thought comes first during that aching moment of despair when a man is brought inside the walls, stripped of his civilian clothes, and forced to stand naked and ashamed while impassive guards examine his body for hidden weapons, drugs, or other contraband. Perhaps it is later, when he follows the herd into one of the great stone blocks and hears the locks turning, inexorably, in a thousand barred and dim-lit cells. Perhaps it is still later, an eternity later, when he thinks he cannot face another dawn in that town of shadows. And there are even those who, on the very eve of parole, run away in wild panic because they unconsciously resist a freedom that holds only uncertainty and fear. Fortunately for all concerned, escape to most prisoners is only a shapeless dream that time and nature eventually dissolve. But in others it does not die. I know that tonight some brooding man tosses in his bunk, planning a break. I know that out in the big yard and around the grounds a few men watch the guards pacing the high walls and time their movements. I know that out on the prison water-front area a prisoner gazes wistfully at San Francisco Bay, wondering whether he can swim the narrow channel close to the San Quentin shore. And I know that in the cells and the jute mill and the furniture shop and other favorite places there may be hidden knives, ropes, crude blackjacks, even guns, waiting for the right day, the crucial moment. And then—though I hope and we all continuously work against it—there may be trouble, bloodshed, perhaps death.

I learned early in life that escape is a risky, futile, and often brutal business. One windy night in January 1913, for instance, I went to a party at one of our San Quentin homes. As I left our house, which was just inside the east gate, I saw a small boat bobbing on the water below the rocky bank, but it was empty and I decided some fisherman had moored it there for the night. After the party ended, my friend Charlie White and I sat down beside one of the gun towers to gab awhile before going home, and I told him about the strange boat. At that moment all the arc lights went out along our prison main street and the whole reservation was blacked out. It began to rain, and I could hear the guard overhead cussing as he fumbled with a candle. Men were running in the darkness, and when a door banged across the street I knew my father had joined other prison guards on an emergency call. I went home in a hurry. The next day every San Quentin family knew that Herbert Repsold, the burglarizing black-sheep son of a prominent San Francisco couple, and one of our wealthiest prisoners, had broken out. Repsold, who worked in the power substation under the warden's office, had pulled the main switches, pocketed the fuses, and vanished in the stormy night. I told my father about the boat, which some friend must have planted there for Repsold, but it had also disappeared and was never seen again.

Several days later, while I was delivering the San Francisco newspapers on my regular prison route, I stepped into the reception room and nearly knocked over a crude pine coffin resting on sawhorses. There was a body in it, a swollen, unrecognizable heap of flesh and bones, and naturally I recoiled from it.

"What's the matter, boy?" one of the guards said. "Don't you like our pal Repsold?"

Repsold! I was tongue-tied.

"Yeah," he drawled. "Looks like he bumped into a rock before he drowned the other night, and we're keepin' him on exhibition just in case some of the other cons think they can pull the same trick."

I have never been able to erase that grim picture from my mind, and even now, thirty-seven years later, I instinctively cringe a little before I enter the reception room. But during those early days, accompanying my father and others, I learned a great deal about various escape techniques and about trailing fugitives, and have used that knowledge many times since I became warden ten years ago. Johnny Carpenter, later the gruff but kindly Captain of the Yard, took special pains to educate me, probably because I was even then—at the age of fifteen—vowing to marry his pretty daughter Gladys. He pointed out to me the most likely routes prisoners would use to reach the highway, and showed me popular hiding places in and around the prison. "Clint," he would say seriously, "if you ever expect to work here, you got to remember that any strange people going out the gate might be escaping prisoners in disguise, no matter how innocent they look. You got to keep your eyes open."

Then one day Captain Carpenter and I happened to be near the gate when a slim figure whizzed past on a bicycle. "Hey, I know him!" he exploded. "That's Gopher Johnson. What a nerve! C'mon, Clint, we'll get him."

We piled into my father's car, rumbled down the dusty road for a mile or two, and soon caught up with our quarry. "Get off that bike, Gopher!" Captain Carpenter roared. The startled cyclist jammed his brakes so hard that he sailed over the handle bars and landed in a ditch, skinning both elbows and knees. And there he sat, howling mightily and looking more like the twelve-year-old son of a San Quentin neighbor, which he was, than Gopher Johnson, which he was not. "Well," said a subdued Captain Carpenter as we returned with our banged-up "prisoner," "I guess I better get some new glasses."

During the summer, when there was no school, my brothers and I always joined in the man hunt that followed an escape. We would fan out into the hills on horseback or afoot, with my father or some other guard in the lead, and carry on the search until the man was caught. There wasn't much traffic for potential hitchhikers around the prison then, and most fugitives sought refuge in the thick underbrush or slid down into one of the rocky canyons to wait for darkness. We had hiked those hills and hollows a hundred times, our initials and marks were on every other tree, and we knew the places where a man might hide. Very few ever made a clean getaway. But there was never anything personal or revengeful in these pursuits; to my father it was routine, though unpleasant, and to us it was a normal part of growing up in our prison town of San Quentin. As a boy, I could never look at a captured prisoner—bleary-eyed, starved, crushed by his failure and facing an extra five-year term—without feeling somewhat sorry for his shortcomings. There was nothing heroic or inspiring about an escape; on the contrary, some of our man hunts ended on a comic-opera note. Once two men covered themselves with Spanish moss, climbed a tree, and tried to look like branches, but an unfortunate sneeze ruined the camouflage. There was also a man who dug a hole and covered himself with a bush, but a sudden gust of wind snatched it out of his hand just as the guards came along. Another time, while crossing a hillside pasture on the trail of two runaways, my father heard a rustling in the high bushes. He thought the noise came from a neighboring farmer's calves which usually browsed there, and so he called out playfully, "Come out or I'll shoot." To his amazement the missing prisoners stepped out with their hands up, and he was caught with his gun down.

We teased my father about that for a long time, and the words "Come out or I'll shoot" were always good for a chuckle around our house. But now, as the result of a recent incident, it seems the laugh is on me. An inmate named George McRae, who worked on the outside garden crew, failed to check in for the four o'clock count one February afternoon. We followed all the routine procedures—

combed the hills and all buildings, searched his cell and read his mail for possible clues to his plans, warned the police with an all-points teletype bulletin, established road blocks and prepared to flood the state with his identification picture and fingerprint data. At seven o'clock the guard crews completed their roundup of the grounds and I was advised that a portion of the garden adjoining my house was the only area not yet searched. There was a cold rain driving in from the north—good escape weather—and the night was as black as the burned grass on the hills. I slipped on a raincoat, called two of the Chinese inmates assigned to our house, and went outside to prowl the garden with a flashlight. There was an arbor near by, densely matted with ivy, but I didn't see how anyone could hide there. But, just to be doing something while I waited for help, I stuck my right hand into my coat pocket and called out: "Come out, Mac, or I'll shoot." There was a sudden flutter of leaves, and a very soggy McRae plopped out of the arbor right at my feet. My son Jack now tells me, not without a snicker, that he believes this was the first time any warden ever caught an escaper "singlehanded," but I have since wondered what McRae would have done had he known I didn't really have a gun.

It so happens that I am considered a good shot, and I am as familiar with guns as any man who has served in the Marine Corps. But I have deliberately avoided carrying a pistol or even having one available in my car or around the house. My father's experience and my own observation taught me that having guns handy was an invitation to shoot, usually without good reason. I saw many a wall guard taking pot shots at men in the yard because they knew no other way to break up a fight or rule on an argument, and nervous trigger fingers uselessly snuffed out many a life.

To me, guns inside the prison meant a constant show of force, a Damoclean sword dangling over the inmates while they worked, ate, and slept. It has taken almost ten years to eliminate most of these threatening rifles, but the upsurge in morale was worth it. In the jute mill, for instance, there were always three gun guards suspended like uneasy tightrope walkers over the heads of the prisoners. In the nerve-racking clatter of the looms new inmates were quite apt to make some gesture that could be misinterpreted, and the strain on them and the gun guards was almost unbearable. We removed one guard at a time, over the protest of some veteran officers. The same procedure has been followed in the mess halls, the main yard, and the cell blocks. Since that time there has never been an incident which would have merited the use of a gun.

There are still riflemen on some of the wall posts, a few strategically located towers, and in the maximum security sections, but I cannot remember when the last shot was fired. Nevertheless, no one in correctional work is naïve enough to overlook the possibility that some foolish inmate may someday smuggle a pistol into the prison and attempt to use it in going over a wall. There are some men, like Ethan McNabb and Rudolph Straight, who cannot think without a gun in their hands, and they show a nettlesome ingenuity in making or obtaining smuggled revolvers. Several others successfully brought in guns during that same period, notably the tough Cook brothers, Fred and Roy, who came in from San Francisco for robbery.

Roy was an especially dangerous prisoner at the time and spent months in the dungeon for inciting riots, fighting in the yard, or refusing to work. Still later, Warden Holohan caught the brothers with three guns—a Colt .38 automatic and two .38 revolvers—a jackpot find that undoubtedly saved many lives. The boys were locked up in the old stone cells whose walls abutted the condemned cells on the other side of the block, and presumably were under control.

But on the other side of the wall, via that mysterious capillary of communication called the grapevine, four condemned men learned that Roy Cook was a kindred spirit who might contribute ideas or materials toward a wholesale break. The doomed men, none of whom had more than a few months to live, were Louis Lazarus, a tailor with a hobby of bank robbery; Perry Coen, who had brutally murdered his sweetheart's parents; John Joseph Malone, a wife-killer; and Edgar Lapierre, who had ambushed a police officer and shot him to death. These four men were willing to take any risk to beat the gallows, but they needed help, and Cook was their man. In time they contacted him, it seems, through Jim McNamara, one of the participants in the terrible dynamiting of the Los Angeles *Times*. McNamara, a lifer, had been assigned to Condemned Row as a sort of helper and messenger boy, and he had more or less freedom of movement within the walls.

Presently the prison buzzed, as it always does when there's a plot afoot, with rumors of a break that would make the headlines. The prison band, it was said, played louder on certain nights to deaden the sound of digging somewhere near Condemned Row, and there was talk of weapons hidden here and there. Certain prisoners were reported to be making anxious inquiries about the weather forecasts, and in the big yard the masses of men were restless. It was inevitable that the gossip would reach informers, and just as inevitable that Warden Holohan would do something about it. One foggy day just before Thanksgiving he ordered Sergeant Julius Scheppler to take a raiding squad and shake down Condemned Row. They found a tunnel connecting Cell 21 to Cell 22, and a second tunnel from there to Cook's cell, No. 46, on the opposite side. They found the weapons, too—half a dozen dirks honed down to the sharpness of a butcher's blade. The knives were tucked away in one corner of the longest tunnel with ropes, blankets, and spare clothing, and would have been ready to use on the first foggy day. The four condemned men were stunned when their secret was exposed; they had pried away at the brick and stone walls for months, believing that no wagging tongue would deny them this one last round. Malone was hanged a week later, cursing the unidentified stool pigeons to the last, and the other three died at the end of a rope not long afterward. McNamara was transferred to Folsom Prison, remained there for years, and was finally brought back to the San Quentin hospital to die. The Cook brothers served their time, and were paroled just about the time Clyde Stevens solved the problem of smuggling guns into the prison for his unlucky friend Rudolph Straight.

Since I became warden, San Quentin has had its share of attempted or successful escapes, but fortunately none of them was the result of a riot or mass action by the inmates. The first two who tried flight were Joe Hines and Eros

Truitt. They were working on the ranch just outside the wall in November 1942, and they simply walked away to the main north-south highway a mile or so from the prison. They flagged down a bus at the town of Corte Madera, but on the short ride to San Francisco they aroused the suspicions of a fellow passenger. He got off at the Golden Gate Bridge toll plaza and officers there telephoned me. Fifteen minutes later, happily stepping out of the bus at its downtown terminal, Truitt and Hines felt very silly indeed when they were greeted by the police. Things were fairly quiet for more than a year after that episode, but late in December 1943 there came one of those bleak mornings damned so eloquently by General Estell a century ago.

The fog was so heavy we could have corked it up in bottles, and in the yard and around the grounds inmates and guards had to feel their way from place to place. We are always uneasy in this kind of weather because we know there are some men waiting for it, patiently, as the cat waits for the mouse. On this particular Sunday morning—it was the day after Christmas—officers went through the cell blocks before the usual unlocking hour to release men who had passes for early church services. In the group were Austin Redford, Ralph Ward, Lawrence Motari, and Roy Drake, all under twenty-one and known to us as "cocky young punks." As a rule we are not especially liberal with these young, calloused prisoners, because most of them are the product of vicious sidewalk gangs and they come to San Quentin with contempt for our kind of program. They want to be "big shots," despite rebuffs from older and wiser inmates, and they present a vexing disciplinary problem while they are trying out their toughness.

But no matter how thick-skinned they are, we encourage them to take part in the religious program and allow them to attend services.

That morning this quartet started for the chapel, but made a quick detour in the fog and ran down to the baseball field. They squeezed through a hole in one wall, a gap left by workmen installing new pipe lines, and clambered over the high outside wall with rope and a crude scaffold made of lumber they found near the spot. They were not missed until the afternoon count, and by that time were miles away. Redford was ditched by the others before the day ended, and pressed northward alone. He was caught at Fort Bragg, in an isolated section of the northern California coast area, on December twenty-eighth, and, in view of succeeding events, that was a break for him. Ward, Motari, and Drake, heading southeast, went all the way to Mississippi, picking up guns and hot cars along the route. They terrorized hundreds of men and women with a rash of holdups in that state and were finally rounded up in a spectacular gun battle. Swiftly tried and convicted, each of these boys was given a one-hundred-year prison term before they were started back to California. They are now in Folsom, considerably subdued by the chilling knowledge that they will be paroled one day, only to find the Mississippi police waiting to pick them up at the gate for that extra hundred years. This affair was more embarrassing and harmful than I like to admit, because they could not have gotten away without carelessness on our part all along the line, but in the long run it resulted in tighter surveillance and an improved system of handling boys of this caliber.

I have never felt any bitterness toward any of the men involved in escapes, despite the trouble and expense they caused. If anything, I feel I may have been partly to blame because I failed to reach a man's heart, or to make him understand how we are trying to help. Actually there is more resentment among the inmates themselves, because an escape frequently causes loss of privileges, a personnel shake-up, and stricter rules, and many a swaggering truant has come back to a cool reception from his friends in the yard. My attitude toward the whole problem of escape is best illustrated, perhaps, by one of our classic San Quentin stories—I suppose there are variations of it in every penitentiary—about a three-time loser who was earnestly pleading his case with the parole board and telling the members how well he had behaved on his current stretch.

"Good conduct is important, of course," said the chairman. "You are to be commended for that. We are now interested in your future. What do you really want out of life?"

"Mister," said the prisoner fervently, "I don't want anything out of life. I'm already doing that. I just want out of here."

That about sums it up—they all want out, and it's my job to keep them in until their time is served. On the whole I have been fortunate, because of all the men who beat the long odds and broke out of San Quentin, not one is now at large. Some others are still missing—men who wandered away from minimum security assignments, such as our forestry or road-construction camps high in the mountains, or the wartime harvest camps. But they will be caught, too, because today it is almost impossible for a man to assume a completely new identity, as any investigator knows, and detection in most cases is only a matter of time and circumstance. We had one man, for example, who was caught after eighteen years of freedom because he was involved in a traffic accident and his fingerprints were taken. Fortunately for him, he had a good record and was not sent back to prison.

There is also the matter of conscience, which, coupled with fear, often makes men surrender voluntarily. Several times I have been awakened at night by telephone calls from penitent men in distant cities, telling me they are coming back or that they will report to the police wherever I suggest. Nor has any of them ever backed down after the decision was made. One was a clever artist I will call Clyde Boyle, who first came to San Quentin on a rape conviction. He was a faultless prisoner, and his ability was so undeniable that he was granted a parole to the army. Two years later, while on duty in Florida, Clyde got liquored up one night and found himself in jail charged with a sex offense. He served a short sentence there, and then, because a felony committed anywhere is also a parole violation in California, he was held for return to San Quentin. The army, as Clyde tells it, had him in custody, waiting for one of our officers. The army also liked him, it seems. "They escorted me out of town," he says, "pointed to the open road, and said, 'Get going, and if you need money or anything else, let us know.'" He weakened and hurried out of Florida and the clutches of the California pursuers. But his conscience bothered him, and when he reached Chicago he called me on the phone.

"Warden, this is Clyde," he said. "I'm coming home.

Please don't try to have me arrested, because it would embarrass my family, but I'll be there as soon as I can make it."

"That a promise, Clyde?" I asked.

"I promise."

Six days later, dusty and hungry, Clyde came back and served his time. When I last heard from him he was earning a good living with his pens and brushes and had found a wife who believed in him and didn't care how long he had been in prison.

There was also William McManus, who might have made trouble after he got away from the prison ranch one June night in 1946 and hid in the hills until the following evening. He started hitchhiking on the highway, and soon a car stopped to pick him up. The driver was silent for a while, but after a mile or two he said: "Nice night for a walk, eh, Mac?" McManus looked up with a start and recognized Charlie White, my administrative assistant, who just happened to be out for a drive that night. McManus could have made a fight for it, but he was too disgusted with his luck. "Oh, hell," he said. "Take me back to the prison."

I especially recall a farm worker named Joe Bagioli who was sentenced to San Quentin during the summer of 1941. In June a year later he disappeared from one of our harvest camps and successfully eluded the police for the next four years. On January 19, 1946, Joe arrived at San Quentin on a bus, convinced the incredulous gate guard that he was a wanted man, and asked to be locked up.

"Well, Joe," I said, "what brought you back here? You like the place?"

"I didn't finish my term," he said simply.

"Yes—but why did you wait so long?"

"It's like this—the parole board wouldn't let me out when the war started. My brother was drafted and his family needed help. I was no good to him as a prisoner, so I walked out, got a job, and supported his wife and kids. The war's over, my brother is back, and now I finish my sentence. Okay?"

I couldn't argue with that kind of logic, and it must have impressed the parole board too. Joe served only fifteen months more before he was released, and he hasn't been in trouble since. In recent years Gladys and I have gotten into the habit of watching faces wherever we go, on the chance that we might find some of our missing camp men. One I would like to see is Ray West, a young man from a prominent northern California family who was brought to San Quentin in 1931 to be executed for killing a laundryman—he claimed it was accidental—during his first holdup. By some miracle Ray was saved from the gallows, possibly because he had no previous felony record, and there was some evidence that he was goaded into the crime by an unscrupulous girl. I thought there was some good stuff in Ray, and he proved it with a flawless work, conduct, and study record for the next eleven years. Finally I recommended him for a temporary job in a harvest camp as the first step toward a possible parole that would send him back to his four children as a good father and useful citizen. He was in the camp only a few months, then he disappeared, and no one has ever seen him again. He may be dead. He may be living a new life somewhere. I don't know—but he is always on my mind. Just the other day Gladys and I were driving along Van Ness Avenue in San Francisco when we saw a man going into a service station.

Gladys grabbed my shoulder and said, "Who does that look like?"

"Ray West," I said.

I stopped the car, jumped out, and ran after him. But I was mistaken, and that man must have thought I was crazy. I mumbled an apology, returned to the car, and we drove home disappointed and depressed. I hope Ray is alive and that, if he reads this, he will send me some word. He should complete his time in prison and not be a wanted man the rest of his life.

If I knew why certain men, especially those who haven't much time to serve, will suddenly jeopardize their whole prison record and risk an added five-year penalty for a few hours or days of uneasy freedom, I would certainly do something about it. For want of a better name, we call this affliction "parolitis," and occasionally an intelligent man recognizes the symptoms and begs us to keep a close watch on him until his parole day. But most of them do not understand their deeply buried motives, and the remorse of a man who realizes he has double-crossed himself, not us, is a painful thing to see. But if we cannot fathom their minds or anticipate the escape impulse, we can at least try to fill the dragging hours with constructive activities that will keep them in touch with the world and strengthen their resolve to live like decent people. That, among other reasons, is why I decided to install radio headsets in each cell, for nighttime listening, in the face of criticism that from some sources was almost hysterical. When I was appointed warden, the prison was in a turmoil from the scandal that had resulted in the removal of Warden Court Smith and the prison board. There were only two hundred and twenty-six guards, officers, and administrative employees to operate an institution bursting with over five thousand men. The inmate activity program was disorganized, the educational system was inadequate because we were limited to daytime classes and inmate teachers, and the men were spending too many hours in their cells with nothing to do. Consequently there were disturbing incidents in the cell blocks—fist and knife fights, suicide attempts, gambling, a rash of thefts. The new hobby-shop program was still in the wishful-thinking stage, and even that would not interest all the men. And, finally, I had known since my boyhood that one of the principal causes of bitterness among imprisoned men is that invisible barrier—much more impregnable than a mere concrete wall—between them and the outside world. I couldn't let them out, but I could bring the world inside with radio.

It seemed like a sound solution to a critical problem, but I was discouraged when I looked around for equipment. The war in Europe was under way, and in America, with factories shifting over to military production, material shortages were already noticeable. I also knew I could not use state money for this project, and I wasn't sure whether the inmate fund could afford it. But we were lucky. After weeks of scouting around, we found a company in San Francisco that agreed to sell us seven thousand headsets and install a large receiving unit at a bargain price of around ten thousand dollars—which was paid entirely by the inmates' own money from their Welfare

Fund. Then we ran wires with jacks attached into every one of our three thousand cells, with most cells having two sets of earphones. Some of my wry-humored friends made the obvious crack that if I really wanted to inflict a terrible punishment I would force all misbehaving inmates to hear nothing but singing commercials all day. There was also an editorial in the San Francisco *News* which said in part:

> *We hope that whoever tunes the programs will spare the poor cons the pain of listening to a lot of soap operas that fill so many radio hours. We can think of no better way to drive a man stir-crazy. But seriously—what will be the effect of listening . . . to the world of free men? Will it be to still the savage breast of caged men and make them more tractable? Or will it create a sense of unrest, an intense resentment against the shackles . . . a determination to make a break for it?*

I couldn't have answered those questions at the time, but the radio system is far beyond the experimental stage now, and rather than causing any unrest, it has contributed much to good discipline and morale. Programs are selected by an inmate committee on the basis of occasional votes cast by all the men, and the final selections are submitted for my approval. Naturally we do not pick up any crime or blood-and-thunder programs—one old-timer says he can hear more exciting yarns out in the yard any day—but there are seldom any other prohibitions. News, music, and comedy are the most popular shows, of course, but there is also a strong and understandable interest in religious presentations, as well as educational programs and dramatic shows. Aside from any other factors, the radio system has had a potent effect on cell-block behavior. Most men listening to their favorite programs at night are too preoccupied to get into a fight or to waste time worrying about themselves. Another thing, when a man is guilty of misconduct, we simply take the headset out of his cell, and that, together with the loss of other privileges, is punishment that really hurts.

Shortly after the headsets were installed, we realized that we might want to originate broadcasts in the prison, such as sports and educational programs, church services, quiz shows, and other special events. Also, of course, it would be a good thing if we could reach all the men simultaneously, in case of an emergency, without bringing them down into the auditorium. I put microphones in my office, my home, and other points throughout the prison, and that was the beginning of San Quentin's "Gray Network." I had been using it only a few weeks when a call came from the U. S. Forest Service late one night, begging us for help in fighting a serious blaze in the mountains. The sleeping inmates were signaled by flashing lights in the cell blocks. I picked up the mike on my desk and then called for volunteers. I told them it would be dangerous work, that they would have but few guards—this was during the war—and that I counted on them not to let San Quentin down. Hundreds offered to go, guards submitted a list, and before 1 A.M. we had two hundred picked men loaded into trucks for the three-hundred-mile journey to the burning forest. Many of those men had not been outside the walls for years; many others had no hope of an early parole.

But they did the job—and they all came back. As a result of their work, both forest services—state and federal—suggested a string of permanent and seasonal conservation camps to be manned by prisoners. The California legislature passed a bill in 1943 to establish the camps in forest areas, and they have been in operation ever since. The men who live in the camps—there are usually about five hundred every year—build trails, fight fires, blister rust, and erosion, and aid in reforestation. Each group works under the supervision of the Forestry Service, with prison officers assigned to the camps for management and off-hour control. Working and living outdoors in comparative freedom presents a great temptation to these men, and although our selection is a careful one, I am never very surprised when one of them cracks up and sneaks away during the night. When such a man escapes I am forced to the conclusion that he wasn't ready for the responsibility and that perhaps our judgment was at fault. Considering the opportunities for escape, we are encouraged by the relatively small number of men who break the trust. A recent tabulation shows the following figures:

	1947	1948	1949
Men to camps	821	605	761
Escaped	12	14	8
Percentage of escapes	1.46	2.31	1.05
Recaptured	10	13	8

On the whole, the camps have made an enviable record, and the chosen prisoners have not only saved millions of dollars' worth of our California forests but they have also salvaged something from their own burned-out and eroded past.

The Gray Network was so effective in reaching the men that I started a question-and-answer program of my own called "Interview Time." I promised I wouldn't duck any problems, and to encourage frankness I told the men they could write me unsigned notes and drop them into a locked box placed in the main yard for that purpose, or mail them to my office in a sealed envelope. This program, with some inevitable side-line needling about my guaranteed Hooper rating, has been fed into the cells approximately twice a month for some seven years now. Men who would never have the nerve to come to my office or approach me in the yard have used Interview Time to tell me about prison problems of all kinds. I have been tipped off to thefts, bribery, food waste, surly employees and troublesome inmates, unsanitary habits, and a hundred other items that I might miss ordinarily. In prison all molehills are mountains, and so I try to answer every question, no matter how ridiculous or trivial. Here are some verbatim excerpts from one of my recent broadcasts:

Q. Warden, here's a man says he's a big eater and wants to know why he can't get seconds.
A. If everybody got seconds, there wouldn't be enough to go around.
Q. There is some guy throwing spitballs in the mess hall, and one landed in my coffee.
A. We ought to get that fellow on the basketball team. But, seriously, we'll keep a closer watch.
Q. Can I establish a private gymnasium in the locker

room of the shop where I work? I have all the necessary apparatus.

A. Hasn't this fellow enough work to do? Better look him up and give him a job.

Q. This man says he misses the 10 P.M. news broadcast because he is in a class, and wants to know if it can be recorded and rebroadcast.

A. Too expensive to do that. And, anyway, he's getting more out of his class than he will from that broadcast.

Q. Here's a man wants to go home for a couple of days to attend a funeral.

A. I'm sorry, but the state law does not allow it.

Q. Half a dozen men in the east block want to know why they have to listen to a fellow who keeps them awake all night playing a guitar.

A. He obviously has no consideration for others. We have a music hour each evening for the playing of instruments. We'll take care of it.

Q. Three men have written to ask why they are allowed to read murder mysteries here but can't have them on the radio.

A. Somebody's slipped up here. I don't know where those men got their murder mysteries, but I suggest they turn them in right away and we'll overlook it this time. Such books and magazines are contraband.

Q. This fellow says every time he gets new jeans, they get lost in the laundry. Says he isn't the only one.

A. Yes, I know. We got a new laundry superintendent

yesterday and have asked him to establish a better system.

Q. This man says he's tired at the end of the day and can just barely make the stairs to the fifth tier. He wants escalators installed in the cell blocks.

A. If he's old or not strong enough, we'll move him to the first tier. Otherwise I'm afraid he'll have to hike it.

To the outsider some of these replies may sound flippant, but I have tried to keep the program on an informal plane because that is basically the relationship I have had with the men since I became warden. There is so little light behind a prison wall that any chink in the mortar gives a glow that lasts for a long time. I found out, for instance, that the man who suggested the escalator was entirely serious, but the rest of the men guffawed about his idea for days, and ever since he has been known as "Escalator Joe." I often suspect that some of the prison clowns plant phony questions just to hear my answers, but I don't begrudge them whatever amusement the program might bring, along with its serious side.

Once in a while I have a chance to change the routine when a distinguished visitor drops in unannounced and accepts my invitation to talk to the men over our network. Edgar Bergen came one evening, and I took him to the control room in the guards' dormitory building. "Edgar doesn't have Charlie McCarthy with him tonight," I said to the men listening in their cells, "but he wants to say hello anyway."

Characteristically, Bergen was inarticulate without

his wooden alter ego, and fumbled badly. "I'm glad . . . glad to be here," he said. "I . . . er . . . hope you have been listening to my . . . uh . . . program."

He stopped talking abruptly, cupped his hand over the microphone, and looked at me appealingly. "I don't know what to say," he whispered. "What should I say?"

"Anything you like," I said. "Tell them about Charlie."

The man who has entertained millions of people for fifteen years without a trace of mike fright gave a shrug of despair and shot a quick glance around the studio. Finally he whipped a handkerchief from his pocket, wrapped it around his right hand, and faced the microphone confidently.

"Well, well," he said, "here comes Charlie. Say something to the boys, Charlie."

"Bergen," the makeshift Charlie quipped, "I've seen you in front of plenty of bars, but this is the first time I've seen plenty of bars in front of you."

"Charlie!"

"Heh-heh, Bergen finally got a wrong number he can't hang up on."

Bergen carried on this patter for half an hour without Charlie and without a script, a twenty-five-thousand-dollar performance that had the men in hysterics and, if I may so, certainly took the edge off the Warden Duffy show the following week. Another time I brought over Tommy Harris, a popular San Francisco singer and night-club owner, to entertain the men on the network. Just as he arrived, two inmates escaped, the siren screamed, and guards were rushing in every direction. Tommy was lost in the scramble, and when I finally got him into the studio a couple of hours later I said, "I'm sorry, Tommy, it's too late for you to sing now. Say good night to the men and tell them you'll be back another time."

Tommy clutched the mike grimly and said: "I don't think I'll be back at all, fellows. I know why those two characters went over the hill. They knew I was going to sing tonight and they couldn't take it."

There's an interesting phenomenon in connection with these intramural broadcasts that professional radio performers notice almost at once. When a top artist performs in a regular network studio he does not have any sharp mental picture of his unseen audience and usually "plays" to whatever people happen to be right there. But these same actors tell me that when they appear on the Gray Network they seem to be looking right into the cells and can almost make out men's faces. I have no explanation for this illusion unless—as I have told them kiddingly —they have a guilty conscience. I have also been gratified to have great movie "gangsters," such as Edward G. Robinson, tell me with mingled surprised and disappointment that San Quentin is unlike any cinema penitentiary they ever saw.

One famous star said to me: "Well, Clint, I have certainly been disillusioned today."

"You mean because we didn't have a couple of murders or maybe a tiny riot?"

"Well . . . yes, I suppose that's what I mean. I went around expecting to see a lot of mean-looking guys hatching up something in the yard, or maybe a hard-boiled guard rapping somebody on the knuckles with a leaded club. Why, these fellows all look like regular people, not like the convicts that were in my prison picture."

"They *are* regular people," I said, "and if you can remember that you'll have a whole new perspective on crime and prisons."

The Gray Network, among other things, also tamed one of the most dangerous murderers we ever had in San Quentin. Or perhaps I should say Gladys did. One spring some years ago a homesick youngster—he was only eighteen—wrote a note to Mrs. Duffy and asked her to say something to the men on Mother's Day. We were hesitant about it at first, because we thought it would be a great responsibility and perhaps a little presumptuous. Neither of us believes in preaching to the inmates—we have lived in Prison Town too long for that—and we know that most of the men resent anything with a Pollyanna tinge. But we thought it might help this boy, and some of the other lonely men who had not had a personal word from a woman in years. So when the time came, Gladys spoke to the men from a microphone in our home. It wasn't a speech, or a talk with a message. It was just a friendly greeting from a woman who had lived in San Quentin all her life and who knew what prison meant to a man who never got a call to the reception room or a letter from a mother, wife, or sweetheart. Immediately after that broadcast went into the cells, Gladys was deluged with letters of gratitude, and many a man addressed her as "Mom." She could not answer all the letters, but I conveyed her thanks on one of my broadcasts and said I hoped she would talk to them again soon. But one of the prisoners wasn't satisfied, and he continued sending letters with his name and number, pleading for a reply.

"Who is this Alfred Wells who writes to me all the time?" Gladys asked me one day. "Do you know him?"

"I should say I do," I said. "He's giving me a bad time. I wish you'd answer him."

I wasn't exaggerating the facts in the least. Alfred Wells was a humpbacked and beady-eyed gnome of a man —he was only about four feet ten inches tall—who had a disposition like an adder and was just as deadly. He had come from San Bernardino, where, some months before, he had been living with his half sister as man and wife. When his older brother Raymond threatened to break up this unhealthy relationship, Alfred calmly decided to wipe out his "enemies." In one hour of horror with his gun, Wells murdered his brother, the latter's wife, and an innocent woman who had the misfortune to be at the Wells home that night. He left their bodies far out in the desert, where he had lured them for the killing, and fled to Nevada, where he was eventually caught.

From the moment Wells arrived on Condemned Row he behaved like a dog with hydrophobia, and we seldom let him loose in the exercise hall. He tried to stab a guard with a dagger made from a bedspring, and after we removed the bed and left him with just a mattress, he turned up with another crude weapon fashioned from a piece of split wood. He ripped open the mattress and threw the padding through the bars, and we had to disconnect the water in his cell because he kept flooding the whole Row. I never saw a man so vicious and so deaf to reason. But Gladys must have touched some wellspring of softness in that unhappy, misshapen human being. He poured out memories of a miserable childhood, of a home without parents, of reform schools, jails, and prisons from coast to coast, and in the telling he apparently suffered a painful metamorphosis. He started a regular correspondence with Gladys, in which he would ask questions about the Bible and she, in turn, made up test questions for him. Like Rattlesnake James, he organized a Bible class and taught many of the other men on Condemned Row. And in the end he found a peace that gave him the strength to die. He told Gladys about it in a note written just a few minutes before he was placed in the chair:

Dear Mother Duffy [he said],

By the time you receive this letter I will be resting in glory. I have no fear of anything that lies ahead, as I know that all is well with my soul and that the Lord will never forsake me. I have really enjoyed all your fine letters, but there is nothing more you can do for me. Give my love to Warden Duffy and thank him for me. I hope you will forgive this poor letter, but I am in a hurry and want to have a little talk with Jesus . . .

At the time I was curious about what it was that made Alfred Wells so bitter and rebellious when he first came to the Row. He didn't tell me for quite a while, but finally it came out. Some years before, Wells had been in San Quentin on a lesser charge. He was assigned to a construction crew, and in March 1938 they put him on a special job. He did his work well, too, and was proud of it. And the thing he helped to build that year was the very instrument that would end his life—the little green room with the lethal-gas chair.

Gladys and I, and some of our San Quentin friends, have done everything the law allows—and perhaps a little more—to lift the melancholia that hangs over Condemned Row. No men are more completely deserted and friendless, on the average, than those awaiting execution; they feel unwanted and despised. I don't think any man should die without a friend, and when there is no one else, Gladys and I are happy to substitute. A year or two ago there was a Negro named Maxwell Bowie on the Row, and it was clear that no power on earth could save him. Max was twenty-three years old, a product of the New Orleans slums who had come to California during the war and who was convicted of shooting a taxicab driver in Oakland. He, too, heard Gladys speak on the Gray Network, and she wrote to him several times, but, for reasons we did not understand at the time, he never replied.

Max had no relatives who cared whether he lived or died, and when other men on the Row had visitors, he watched them enviously and sobbed quietly in his cell. One morning in November, Gladys learned that Max was having a birthday, and, as a surprise for the boy, she ordered a large birthday cake and sent it to him with a greeting card. It was the first and last birthday party Max ever had—indeed, it was the first on Death Row—and Max shared the cake with the other condemned men. We had a song dedicated to him on the Gray Network, and they sang it with him, and for just a little while that afternoon there was forgetfulness up there in that dark world. Max is gone now, but I still have the letter he sent to Gladys after the party:

Dear Mrs. Duffy:

All of us on the Row thank you from the bottom of our hearts for making my birthday a memorable one in-

stead of a depressing experience, which it would have been but for your kindness in sending me that lovely letter which heralded the arrival of a masterpiece of a cake, and a number dedicated to me on the Gray Network.

The letter will be a symbol of uplift and the tasty memory of the birthday cake will be an added beauty to a life that has had ugly moments. All admired the cake, particularly the superb lettering: "Birthday Greetings, Maxwell." All this has perhaps made us better men to some degree. God bless you . . .

Maxwell Bowie

Some man's tears were spilled on that letter, and the ink was dissolved and ran across the paper. I still don't know who composed its flowery sentences. It wasn't Max Bowie. He had never learned to read or write.

8 Because the human mind is so unpredictable, I have to remind myself quite often that San Quentin is still a prison, still a place where men are locked up every night, still a house of intrigue whose black sheep can revolt and bring on sudden death any day.

I am always apprehensive on moonlight nights, for instance, because that is when the unstable prisoner seems to crack up. I am not superstitious or a believer in lunar influences, but the full moon almost invariably starts a chain reaction of disorder. In a matter of hours on one of those silvery nights two inmates punched guards, another made a deadly knife, several refused to obey orders, two more were mixed up in fist fights, and one attempted to murder his cellmate. Even one of the guards slipped up —he fell asleep in his watchtower with a gun between his knees, and we had to wake him by throwing rocks at his window. We usually dismiss such men at the first offense, incidentally, because the moment a guard is labeled a "sleeper" by certain inmates, they begin to appraise him for other useful weaknesses. There are smugglers, for instance, who attempt to bribe guards for liquor, drugs, guns, or other contraband. If bribery fails, and usually it does, this small minority of incorrigibles will take bold chances to get what they want. On my desk now, for example, is a box of new tennis balls which were sent to one of our men—they are used in handball games—by a friend outside. One of our officers tested the balls, and when the first one didn't bounce properly he ripped it open. It was stuffed with benzedrine, until recently the favorite prison drug because it was the cheapest way to go on a jag. We had a great deal of trouble with benzedrine preparations for many months, in fact, mostly because the drug was readily obtainable in pharmacies. Shortly after an inmate first discovered that benzedrine dissolved in water was almost as intoxicating as straight whisky, prison smugglers began importing the drug in some quantity. Two or three times we caught employees in benzedrine deals with prisoners, and some men took so much of the drug that they began having hallucinations. The situation became so serious that, at the request of the Department of Corrections, the state legislature amended a section of the penal code, making it a felony for anyone to bring benzedrine into a state prison. We put up large signs at the east entrance gate warning all visitors about this rule, but that did not deter some women from carrying inhalers—innocently or not—in their handbags. We spotted a number of them on the viewing screen of our Inspectoscope—an X-ray device used for routine examination of visitors—but usually let the women go with a scolding, after confiscating the inhaler and destroying it. Now, of course, the benzedrine manufacturers have altered the formula of the drug so that it no longer has any intoxicating effect.

In earlier years there was an alarming traffic in morphine, heroin, cocaine, and other drugs, but we rarely find it nowadays. There was one case, however, involving an inmate with literary ambitions. He was ordering boxes of bond paper direct from a manufacturer, as was then allowed by the rules, and he seemed to be a very prolific writer. Finally, when one of our officers read some of the stuff and concluded that no sane editor would buy it, he became suspicious and had the man's typing paper analyzed. It was saturated with morphine.

There will always be a few men who will take a long chance to get some contraband item, and those few have forced us to insist on rigid control of the mails. Our staff in the mail department handles some fifty thousand letters, packages, and telegrams every month, and each piece is carefully read or examined. We find love letters, fragrant with perfume, which are so suggestive that they would demoralize or torture a prisoner, and we send them back. Others have had invisible lines written with vinegar, lemon juice, or other favorite disappearing inks. The writers invariably expose themselves by leaving unusually wide margins or spaces between the lines, or using instruments which clearly show the disturbed fibers on the paper's surface. As a rule, invisible writing can be brought out by the application of heat or water or, in stubborn cases, by ultraviolet rays. All packages addressed to inmates are carefully inspected, of course, and only a moron would attempt this kind of smuggling. We keep a careful record of every letter written or received by the inmates, and our censors read every line. This is a prodigious book-keeping job, but in the long run it benefits the men themselves. Letters are clues to a man's thinking and his emotions—they show progress or despair; they reveal an unreported illness, a family crisis that has affected a man's behavior, or even evidence that may be vital to his chances for parole. From these records we know the names of an inmate's confidants, information that has been useful in more than one escape.

One case in point involved a young man serving his first prison term, an adversity so overwhelming to him that he couldn't bear it, and he escaped at the first opportunity. Examination of his correspondence disclosed that he had been influenced, more or less, by tearful letters from an older sister who, without realizing the consequences, virtually encouraged him to break out. I telephoned the police in the boy's home town and suggested that they watch the sister's house, because I was sure he would go there. Three hours later, without any attempt at disguise, the fugitive came ambling down the street and was taken into custody at the front door of the house. In cases such as this, where an additional sentence for escape might embitter a prisoner and ruin his chances for early rehabilitation, the parole board considers all the factors. I doubt very much whether this boy understood what he was doing, and his dominating sister was certainly not a good influence. My confidence in him was not misplaced, as it happens; he became a model prisoner and has done very well since his release.

Although almost all men appreciate and protect their reception privileges, some visitors are a problem, and an occasional prisoner who is too smart to use the mails will deliberately make pawns of friends and relatives. Jack Lewis's counterfeit scheme, for example, could not have succeeded without the help of civilians who brought in materials and carried out the spurious currency. The practice of sending or receiving secret messages is called "kiting," and we are on constant guard against it. Sometimes inmates bribe employees to carry out letters, but this calls for such subtlety, patience, and careful negotiation that few men are willing to take the chance. But sympathetic visitors are more amenable, and more than one man or woman has become involved in a plot to beat the contraband rules. In years gone by, those of us in the business have encountered such ingenious things as tear-gas pencils, fountain pens filled with high-proof liquor, cigarettes containing drugs, handkerchiefs steeped in morphine, and family portraits with money or messages concealed in the frame. When holiday packages were allowed, a doting mother now and then sent in a cake well soaked with rum. Also, a tender kiss between a man and his wife might conceal the passing of a capsule filled with drugs or poison or paper money. Gift packages are no longer permitted. We do not have any trouble with our carefully chosen guests who take inspection tours through the prison, but we don't allow them to mingle with the inmates. The most common violation of the rules is the passage of paper money from visitors to inmates, but we try to avoid this and similar kiting by carefully searching every prisoner before and after his trip to the reception room.

Despite our constant vigil, we cannot entirely eliminate contraband articles, and the search for them is endless and is carried on every day somewhere in the prison. Five guards usually compose the shakedown squad, and they go into a shop or a cell block without warning. They examine everything—books, papers, boxes, work clothes, tools, and materials. They look under carpets and staircases, they tap walls and floor boards. They always find something. A typical yield would include a knife or two, coffee or sugar stolen from the commissary, cooking utensils of different kinds, forbidden tools, lewd pictures or drawings, extra clothing, unreported library books, homemade brass knuckles, a little silver or paper money. One recent shakedown in a cell block turned up a book entitled *Ace in the Hole*. Our civilian librarian, Herman Spector, said he was delighted that the long-lost book was found because there had been a demand for it. We were delighted too—because inside the book we found a hacksaw. I told an official from another institution about this hacksaw incident one day, and he interrupted me to say: "We had a man like that, too, but I'll bet he won't do it again. We locked him up in a dark cell, gave him bread and water for two weeks, and took away his privileges for three months."

"That's rough punishment for that," I said.

"Rough?" he snapped. "You should see what they get for something really serious. Clint, you can be too easy on some of these fellows."

The old-fashioned conception of punishment dies hard, and, as John Wilkins painfully learned half a century ago—and it is still true in some minds today—too many people feel that the state should take physical revenge on its incarcerated felons. I could not be a prison warden today, or any time, if I had to solve my disciplinary problems with the strap, the rubber hose, dungeons, strait

220

jackets, and other corporal means. I think we fail as human beings if we cannot reach a man with a constructive prison program geared toward his rehabilitation, a program of reason and logic which offers him a good future if he behaves.

This does not mean that there is no punishment in San Quentin. There is. And I think it is much more effective than the old-time brutality. In place of the dungeon, for instance, we have the isolation cells, jocularly known to the inmates as "Siberia." These cells are on the top floor of the north cell block, in the same wing as Condemned Row, and are similar to the cells in the other blocks. Each cell is equipped with a single bed, toilet and washbowl, blankets and electric light, but no personal belongings are allowed. Meals are served twice a day—it is the same food received by other inmates—and they are allowed to have coffee and tea. We haven't put a man on bread and water in years, and even the most pugnacious prisoner gets nothing worse than "Siberian meat loaf." Housewives interested in a balanced diet might like to have our recipe for this dish:

> *2 oz. powdered milk*
> *3½ oz. raw grated potato*
> *1 oz. tomato puree*
> *3½ oz. chopped carrots*
> *3½ oz. chopped cabbage*
> *4 oz. ground beef*
> *2 oz. lard or shortening*
> *5 oz. red beans precooked*
> *1 oz. white or whole-wheat flour*

½ oz. table salt
1 tablespoon chopped onion
1 egg
½ oz. chili powder

We shape all these ingredients into a loaf, bake it, and serve it twice a day with whole-wheat bread. It is also known as the monotonous diet. I doubt whether Duncan Hines would recommend this dish, but it furnishes twenty-five hundred calories a day and is adequate to maintain full health and vigor. Two or three days of the meat-loaf meal are usually enough to improve the behavior of a man who likes to eat, and the effect is likely to be lasting. If you ever have a guest in your home who pales if you merely mention the words "meat loaf," he could be a San Quentin grad.

But, you may ask, is this the only punishment—a few days in a solitary cell? Obviously it is not. The real punishment lies in the loss of cherished privileges, for there is nothing in solitary but a man and his thoughts. There is no companionship. There are no books except the Bible; there is no radio headset. He cannot write or receive letters or see visitors except under special circumstances. He is away from his daily work assignment and his friends, he misses the weekly movie show and loses his Canteen privilege. He can't attend the prison basketball or baseball games, and he is barred from his work in the hobby shop. I have known men, I am sure, who could absorb physical punishment without a quiver—if we used it—but who cannot take the loss of these small pleasures and will work feverishly to regain their privilege cards. Solitary confinement, of course, is inflicted only in the more serious violations, and the average stay is only five days. Department of Corrections rules specify a thirty-day limit for any inmate in isolation, except in the case of a man who might jeopardize the safety of others if he is released. Such cases are rare and usually involve incorrigibles who will be transferred to Folsom Prison, or psychopathic inmates scheduled for removal to a state hospital. The average stay in isolation is only eight days.

In San Quentin, where five thousand men are confined in relatively close quarters, minor fights and disturbances can be the fuse that will set off a major explosion. Consequently these violations must be quietly handled on the spot or, in any case, within twenty-four hours. Evidence is heard by a disciplinary court composed of myself, Associate Warden of Custody Harley Teets, Associate Warden of Care and Treatment Douglas Rigg, Dr. David Schmidt, our chief psychiatrist, and Lieutenant Dan Coughlin, or an alternate from any of these departments. Let's look in on one of these hearings for a moment. We are seated around a desk in Teets's office, which faces the quadrangle formed by the San Quentin garden, and the offending inmates are lined up outside waiting their turn. The first case involves a young fellow who comes in with downcast eyes and a cringing attitude that says, "I won't get a break."

TEETS: What's the problem here, Lieutenant?
COUGHLIN: He's been throwing bread away in the mess hall. Wasting a lot of it. Refuses to eat it after he's taken it.

TEETS: The record card indicates he's a renegade. Is that true?

INMATE: Yes, sir. Guess I've been a troublemaker.

TEETS: Well, you used to get charged about once a month. Maybe you're growing up now?

INMATE: I'm trying. I just couldn't eat that bread. I had too much.

TEETS: You just didn't think. Why risk trouble for one slice of bread?

DUFFY: I would have eaten that slice, son, with a parole dangling in front of me. You were wasting bread. If every man wasted food, there would not be enough to go around.

INMATE: I couldn't do it.

DUFFY: Even in an emergency?

INMATE: No, sir.

TEETS: How about a sixty-day probation for this infraction?

DUFFY AND RIGG: All right.

The next case is a dark, sultry-looking youth with a jutting chin, a teen-age prodigal from a slum district in one of California's larger cities. His record card shows thirteen previous violations, most of them committed in an attempt to show older inmates how tough he is. He has been caught gambling in the jute mill with a deck of prison-made cards, and he is also wearing his hair thick and long at the back of his neck, in the "drugstore cowboy" style.

TEETS: Johnny—where did you get that haircut?

JOHNNY: Right here.

TEETS: You haven't been to the barbershop recently. You know what the regulation haircut is.

JOHNNY: Aw, I got it here.

DUFFY: You're not telling the truth about the haircut. You're not even trying to stay out of trouble. You know playing cards are not allowed.

JOHNNY: Yes, sir.

TEETS: What do you plead?

JOHNNY: Not guilty.

TEETS: Sure you don't want to change that plea?

JOHNNY: Well, I'll plead guilty to having cards. But I don't gamble.

DUFFY: The record shows you've gambled before.

JOHNNY: Yeah?

DUFFY: You've also got a tattoo mark under your eye. You had that put on before you came here, didn't you?

JOHNNY: It isn't anything. Some of the Mexicans do it.

DUFFY: Johnny, I've been around here quite a while. That's a gang insignia, isn't it?

JOHNNY: Yes.

TEETS: I suggest sixty days' loss of privileges. Okay?

ALL: Okay.

The third case on the morning's calendar involves a muscular young man from Louisiana who started a fight in the mess hall during the evening meal. He is shaking a little, and his big hands curl and uncurl, and there is a slight bruise on his face below the high cheekbone.

TEETS: Jimmy, I guess you know how serious this is?

JIMMY: Yes, sir, but that other guy——

TEETS: Just a minute until I finish. There were over two thousand men filing into the mess hall when you started this ruckus. Do you realize what could have happened?

JIMMY: No, sir.

TEETS: In one minute you could have started a riot, and there's no telling what might have happened. Why did you hit him?

JIMMY: I don't rightly know. He was behin' me, makin' dirty cracks.

TEETS: About what?

JIMMY: Well . . . about my home town.

TEETS: And that's reason enough for you to hit him? You were willing to lose all your credits and privileges for that?

JIMMY: Does sound kinda for nothin' at that.

TEETS: You bet it does. Did you ever hear of Big Joe?

JIMMY: You mean that fella up on Condemned Row?

TEETS: Yes, that's the one. He started a fight just like you did. One of the guards tried to stop him, and he nearly killed the man. He was a lifer—just like you are. He's sentenced to die for what he did.

JIMMY: Well, Jezuss! I wasn't gonna kill nobody.

TEETS: You don't know what you were going to do. Think it over. Ten days in solitary. Okay, Warden?

DUFFY: Fair enough. You're lucky the fight wasn't any worse, Jimmy. Stay out of trouble and do your own time. We don't want to see you in here again.

JIMMY: Yes, sir.

And so it goes, one case after another. Men with strong tempers, men with hate, men who make mistakes and admit it. In every case we have to administer a kind of frontier justice; we believe that our verdicts are fair, and I think most of the men involved would agree. I think we could take any group of five thousand free men, men without criminal records, and find the same percentage of violators if they, too, were suddenly snatched out of their private world and locked up behind barriers of steel and stone. Imagine yourself living in the finest suite in America's most luxurious hotel, with all your clothes, meals, books, entertainment, and other things furnished, on one condition—that you do not step outside the hotel. You might like it for a few days, or a week, or even a month. But do you think you could stand it for a year, or five years, or life? You could not. You, too, would curse, and get into fights and refuse to work, and scheme about some safe way to break out. Under the circumstances, I am truly amazed at the small percentage of men who break the rules. We do not average more than sixteen to eighteen men in solitary at any one time, and only two or three of them are in real trouble.

There are many other types of disciplinary problems, including those inmates who, despite the fact that they are well fed, try to do a bit of cooking or coffee-making in their cells or some remote corner of one of the shops. The shakedowns often yield crude pots, made from miscellaneous materials picked up around the prison, and no one is surprised when the same raid turns up pieces of bread or toast. There is nothing seriously wrong with these practices—it's a prison form of icebox raiding—but if we allow

227

one man to get away with it, all the rest have a legitimate complaint. It also poses a health problem. San Quentin is a big place. One cell block alone is a maze of one thousand cells, a five-story building about twice as long as a football field, and it is not easy to control ants, cockroaches, or mice if they nose out food hoards.

There are the home-brew artists, too, who attempt to convert stolen sugar, raisins, candy, fruit juice, or other materials into liquor, often with disastrous effects. Two years ago, as a case in point, two prisoners who had been in San Quentin for years succeeded in making some raisin wine in a tool shed. One of the officers smelled the mash, reported to me, and guards were sent down to bring the men to the captain's office. Meanwhile, panicky over the discovery of their alcoholic cache, the two men escaped from their assignment outside the walls. Three days later they showed up in Klamath Falls, Oregon—driving a stolen car and armed with stolen guns. They held up a service-station man, but were spotted almost immediately afterward by police in a prowl car. In the gun battle that followed, one of them surrendered, but the other, wounded, crawled away in the darkness and got as far as Arkansas before he was caught. I knew him well, a man who had come to San Quentin with a death sentence and who worked his way to a position of trust after Governor Merriam saved him from the gallows. There wasn't a black mark against his record in more than twelve years, and he had been to harvest and forest camps five times without making a move to escape.

"What happened, Al?" I asked him when he was brought back. "Why did you do this?"

"I don't know exactly, Warden," he said. "For no reason at all I decided I just had to have a drink. We made that wine, and when I heard it was discovered I just went to pieces and took off."

That one drink cost this man all his credits, a conviction on a new robbery charge, and at least an additional five years for escape. The other men in San Quentin are all familiar with this case, but the big price Al paid does not seem to deter the few confirmed alcoholics from occasionally trying to manufacture intoxicants. Alcohol, indeed, has been the silent instigator in an appalling number of crimes, and in one of our surveys at San Quentin some years ago sixty-eight per cent of the men admitted, or their records revealed, that liquor had played some part in their downfall. I was discussing this one day with Archie Lyons, then a member of the parole board, and he said he, too, was disturbed by the increasing number of cases in which men were drunk when they committed a crime or had drinking trouble while on parole.

"Archie," I said, "what's wrong with San Quentin having an Alcoholics Anonymous chapter?"

"Not a thing, Clint," he said. "If you want to start it, I'll help you."

The Alcoholics Anonymous movement was in its infancy then, but I communicated with some of the organizers in San Francisco and they agreed to come to San Quentin. No other prison had ever tried A.A. within the walls, and there was some official apprehension because we would have to bring in civilians to work closely with our men. Nevertheless, we took the chance, and we got our first twenty members by announcing the A.A. program and its purpose in the San Quentin *News* and over the Gray Network.

The men who founded the prison A.A. chapter sacrificed many of their pleasures and much of their time to recruit new members and keep them in line. Later, when there was a real tragedy involving fourteen known alcoholics, the A.A. men dispelled all doubts about their sincerity and the value of the program. The emergency began shortly before 4 A.M. one October morning, in one of the old Spanish prison cells. An officer, hearing someone crying for help, found inmate Joseph Davis buckled up on the floor of his cell. He was gasping for breath and seemed to be in great pain, but there was no evidence of any injury. At almost the same hour, in the north block, guards on the night shift found two other men, John Genoese and Robert Henderson, writhing in agony. All three were taken to the hospital, and before dawn were joined by four others. The first three couldn't talk coherently, but the others admitted they had all been drinking the fluid used in our duplicating machines. This preparation contains both grain and wood alcohol, plus other commercial solvents, and they could not have picked a more virulent cocktail.

"Warden," Henderson gasped when I tried to talk with him at the hospital, "you better get the others. A bunch of us drank this stuff."

"Who are they?"

"I don't know their names. I can't remember anything . . . I feel like I'm on fire . . . it's getting dark . . ."

Henderson and Davis went blind and died very quickly, and the doctors worked frantically to save the rest. I went to the microphone in my office and broadcast a warning message into the cells.

"Two men have just died in the hospital from drinking printing fluid," I said. "Two others are very ill and may die. Somewhere in the prison there are other men who drank this same stuff. I urge you to report to the hospital immediately. Don't worry about any punishment. Your lives are at stake. I repeat. All those who drank printing fluid last night report to the hospital immediately. Your lives are at stake."

A.A. men who heard this broadcast promptly volunteered to help, and before long the other drinkers began straggling into the hospital, white with fear and the strain of having tried to conceal the burning pains they felt. There has never been such a grim night in the hospital, with two men already dead, two more dying, and ten others in various stages of agony. With nineteen A.A. men helping, the overworked doctors administered glucose, oxygen, penicillin, ice packs, digitalis, blood transfusions, and other emergency treatment. Genoese and Ottis Clark, both young men, fought death for two days before they succumbed, but the others were saved. I think the lucky ten owe their recovery not only to Dr. Alex Miller and his staff but also to the A.A. members who worked with them day and night, donating blood, foregoing meals, and giving up their few pleasures so that these unfortunate drinkers might live.

The A.A. movement has been in full swing for the past seven years, with an average membership of two hundred men, and on Sundays our men have worked with as many as one hundred A.A. visitors from Berkeley, San Jose, San

231

Francisco, Oakland, Richmond, Vallejo, San Anselmo, and other bay county cities. The free men and women in this remarkable organization have contributed much time and money to help the prisoners. The program has been such a spectacular success that more than fifty other prisons and institutions in the United States, Canada, and Australia have since adopted the San Quentin plan. I believe that A.A. men on parole have a consistently better record than other parolees who do not have such unselfish and devoted moral support from a civilian group. It is too bad, I think, that we cannot have a Forgers Anonymous or a Sex Offenders Anonymous, among others, to help those whose crimes have a repetitive and seemingly incurable pattern.

Lacking such organizations, we have substituted a group know as The Seekers. The idea was suggested by an inmate doing life for murder, an intelligent man who thought that a truthful self-analysis might give him, and others like him, some clue to their antisocial behavior. I thought it was a sound thesis and encouraged him to go ahead. There were only ten inmates in the original group, but now, when they meet on Saturday afternoons with Douglas Short, a member of our staff, there are apt to be from one to two hundred men. They discuss crime and their own criminal behavior frankly, with an almost frenzied eagerness for the truth. Many times they have brought in outside speakers—district attorneys, detectives, newspapermen, social workers, and others—to obtain the public viewpoint. The Seekers help one another, they preach and practice the democratic ideals, and they have contributed their share toward the continuing studies in the field of crime. I feel that many of them are better men for this catharsis. It was a Seeker, for example, who turned in a fully loaded gun—a weapon worth a fortune in any prison—after he found it in a navy uniform sent to our large cleaning plant. It was a Seeker who jumped on a runaway car with an unconscious woman driver and stopped it from crashing into a wall—an act that might have looked like an escape attempt and drawn shots from the nearby Arsenal tower. There were Seekers among the prisoners who risked their lives as guinea pigs in a bubonic-plague serum test, and many a Seeker was decorated for bravery during the fighting overseas. In the real sense of the word, these men are Seekers no longer. They found something that had eluded them all their lives.

9 Somewhere in the world—and I wish I knew just where to look—a wanted man named John Hendricks is hiding out.

He would be about fifty-two years old now, a husky, attractive, and talented man who left San Quentin with a dream and found it a nightmare instead. He has been missing more than two years already, leaving behind him the wreckage of a new life he had begun after serving fourteen years on a murder charge, and sometimes I doubt that he will ever turn up. I am telling the story of John Hendricks on the long chance that he will read this and perhaps return for another try. I am also telling it because he helped me bring about the rebirth of music in San Quentin, an event that was followed by one of the most unusual experiments ever tried behind prison walls.

It began one Sunday afternoon in 1940 when I came down to the broad cement plaza outside the cell blocks to listen to the regular weekly band concert. I had always believed with the poets that "music hath charms to soothe the savage breast," but as I listened to the performance

234

that day I was beginning to have doubts. The inmate musicians wore the traditional somber gray-and-black uniforms and they played as though the parole board had just turned them down. The audience consisted of ten bored civilians and half a dozen sea gulls which swooped overhead and unnerved the players. The next day I called in Ted Stanich, a guard whose professional musical background was going to waste in the jute mill, and asked him to give the band a shot in the arm. Ted hustled around and found an old piano, a couple of battered saxophones, and some dusty fiddles that hadn't been touched for years. We thumbed through the files and got a list of men who could play boogie as well as a military march. And then we called in Hendricks. John had come to San Quentin in 1932 with a life sentence for killing a friend during a drinking bout in Los Angeles County. He was lucky to escape the gallows, as the trial judge said somewhat bitterly at the time, and John's gratitude was reflected in a spotless behavior record. Indeed, he was there two years before someone discovered he had once been an army bandmaster and was a walking encyclopedia of music. He joined the old prison band and handled the baton for a while, but his heart wasn't in it.

"John," I said, "I want a new orchestra that can play what the men inside want to hear. I want an orchestra that will chase the blues out of this place and still be good enough to attract outsiders. Can you do it?"

"I sure can, Warden," he said.

And he did. John coaxed, threatened, and cussed those musicians at rehearsals far into the night, a prison Toscanini who was determined to show that murderers, thugs,

235

and thieves can also have music in their hearts and perhaps play as well as most orchestras outside. I could hardly believe my eyes sometimes, watching certain gangsters and tough guys meekly taking John's caustic rebukes, but they had respect for his musicianship and were anxious to please. John's first jazz concert in the mess hall nearly shook the girders out of the roof, and a stranger might have thought it was a riot. The waiters took up the beat with their big metal spoons, plates were banged on table tops, and the men stomped their feet on the concrete floor. There was such an upsurge of morale inside those ancient walls after the first few concerts that I decided to have the orchestra at the noon meal more often, and sometimes there was an extra performance at night which went into the cells via the newly installed prison radio network. All the inmates were proud of their hard-working band, and that pride was shown in their conduct and their work. Before long, various carefully selected lodges, clubs, and groups of peace officers from nearby towns were invited to hear the band, and word soon spread around about the new spirit in the big house by the bay.

About that time we were making a series of sweeping changes in the prison rules, and many more were on the schedule. We had already closed the dungeons and forbidden all forms of physical punishment. We had eliminated head shaving and the sloppy clothes with their big telltale numbers, and had abandoned some of the gun towers around the hills. We had a bright new prison weekly, a hobby program that was helping the men to earn money, and had opened the Canteen to reduce gambling and a traffic in contraband goods. We had work for every man. Next I wanted to improve the educational and industrial systems so that men would go out into the free world better prepared to support their families. But a prison program, no matter how progressive, is only as good as the support it gets from the government and the people. I wanted to tell the people what we were doing, and I got the brash notion that if we had an all-inmate package show, to use the trade term, we might get it on the air. I was just naïve enough at the time, frankly, not to understand the possible complications of such an idea, otherwise I probably wouldn't have had the nerve. I told Ted Stanich and John Hendricks what I had in mind, and they went to work. They found a young waiter in the mess hall who had a voice like an Irish thrush, and in one of the shops they uncovered a baritone who had been overheard singing Negro spirituals at his work. Ted Stanich held a contest for inmate announcers and picked a young fellow from the business office. An inmate rounded up thirty men who were interested in choral work and started a glee club. We rehearsed the singers with the orchestra for two or three weeks, and then recorded a sample program. I put the platter in my brief case and went to see the manager of one of the most powerful stations in San Francisco. I told him what I wanted, and offered to play the record.

"A bunch of cons on the air?" he bellowed. "I should say not! You must want to get me fired."

I went to another station a few blocks away. The manager there was polite and friendly, but he said he couldn't use our show even if we had Humphrey Bogart in the cast. I tried two more downtown stations, but they didn't want any part of San Quentin. By this time my ardor had cooled considerably, but I was willing to try one more, KFRC, mainly because I had to pass the station on my way out Van Ness Avenue toward the Golden Gate Bridge. To my surprise, the manager, Bill Pabst, listened to me eagerly and said he thought it was a unique and intriguing idea.

"That's great, Bill," I said. "I even have a wonderful theme song for the show—'Time On My Hands.'"

"Oh, lord, no!" he said. "That's out. It would make people mad."

I felt that the song was important to the whole philosophy of the show and I didn't want to give it up. I said I was sorry but that we would try somewhere else.

"Now, wait a minute," he said. "I suppose it really wouldn't hurt. The title might get a laugh. I guess you've made a deal."

San Quentin on the Air, as our show was called, made its debut from the small mess hall in the prison on January 12, 1942. The inmates had worked feverishly to build a new stage and stands for the musicians, and they had used their own funds to buy other necessities—new instruments, soundproofing material, sheet music, wiring, and a shiny new baton for their leader. The San Rafael Sciots lodge had thoughtfully donated colorful uniforms for the band, and the boys in the glee club had begged, borrowed, or bleached—I almost said stolen—enough white shirts and duck pants so they wouldn't look like a rogues' gallery in front of the visitors I had invited to the first broadcast. More than anything else, the five thousand men in San Quentin felt that this was their own show and that they were on trial before the public—and they wanted it to be good. The script called for a two-minute talk from me, and I was more nervous than a lifer up for his first parole hearing. But everything went smoothly, and Pabst phoned congratulations as soon as we signed off.

I'm afraid I got a little sentimental that night. I felt that with the magic of radio we had penetrated the invisible wall that separates imprisoned men from those who judged them, and would judge them again in the outside world. I felt that people with compassion would read between the lines of our script and the verses of our songs and would see prisoners as men who had gone wrong but who would not stay wrong. I felt that I could talk to those millions of homes and say with all my heart: "Ninety-eight per cent of these men are eventually going out—many who will stay out and someday be your neighbors. If they are behaving themselves, accept them, and give them the chance they've earned."

In a matter of weeks San Quentin on the Air spread to more than three hundred stations on Mutual's coast-to-coast network, and the San Quentin post-office staff floundered in a sea of some four thousand fan letters a week. The inmate crooners got so many song requests that our mail censors couldn't cope with the problem. During that first year one performer alone introduced several songs that eventually made the Hit Parade, and thereafter we received from eighteen to twenty-five songs a week from the Tin Pan Alley publishers who wanted them plugged on our show. Unknown to us, one of our regular listeners was Pierre Monteux, the impetuous Gallic conductor of the San Francisco Symphony, and he bustled into the prison unannounced one afternoon while Hendricks was rehearsing his men.

"I heard you conducting your own arrangement of the 'Ballad for Americans,'" he said. "Would you mind if I tried it?"

John handed over his baton with trembling fingers.

"Now," said Monteux with a grin, "we will play."

He stood there for an hour, quietly guiding that dumfounded little group of prison musicians, and when they finally got over the shakes they played as they had never played before. When the impromptu concert was over, Monteux briskly stuffed John's arrangement into his brief case and clapped on his hat. "I am leaving on a vacation," he said to the now limp orchestra. "I will study this and teach it to my men. Thank you all—and good luck."

The San Quentin show was on the air for two and a half years, and during that period, whenever one of our players was paroled, Hendricks used to comfort himself with the whimsical thought that the district attorneys around the state would surely send replacements. Sometimes they did. "You'd think the boys would be glad to come here," Hendricks once said laughingly. "Only place I know where a musician is sure of three meals a day."

Hendricks was particularly worried about the loss of Eddie Jorgan—I'm giving him that name because he is free now—a Negro baritone who was one of the stars of the show. Eddie's favorite song was that popular lament called "Ol' Rockin' Chair's Got Me," but whenever he thought some member of the parole board might be listening, he rewrote the lyrics thus:

> *Ol' rockin' chair's got me,*
> *An' this time it's a thorn in my side,*

Do tell, if I only had a parole, Warden,
Rules and regulations I'd sure abide.
Well, it looks like I jist can't git from dis cabin heah,
It seems like dese folks ain't nevah gon' let me go nowhere;
Jes sittin' roun' heah, wishin' an' thinkin'
How dat Navy or dem shipyards could use me out dere.

Eddie was so persistent with this wail and sang it so low down that the parole board finally weakened and gave him a release date. He worked in the shipyards until the end of the war, and spent his evenings singing without pay for soldiers and sailors in USO centers, and his record for the past four years has fully justified the parole board's faith.

I recall another time when Hendricks, having just lost another good man, pretended to rejoice that one of the best drummers in the land, a man known to every bobby-soxer, had just been convicted of a crime and would soon be available to the San Quentin band. Fortunately the great man got a reversal and went free, and Hendricks, who wouldn't have wished bad luck to any man, admitted he was glad and relieved. We finally ran out of enough top-flight talent and brought the program to an end shortly before the war ended.

Ted Stanich died just a few months ago, and the show itself is only a memory now, but I am grateful for the fact that it enabled me to talk to millions of Americans every week about the hopes and aspirations of all the men in San Quentin. Along with thousands of other inmates, most of the musicians and singers went out into the free world to make good, and John Hendricks got his own parole not long after he published his first popular song. He had a fine industrial job and was reporting to the parole officer regularly, as the law requires. Then one day he failed to report, knowing he could be returned to San Quentin for that dereliction alone, and he has never been seen since. He wrote to me just before he disappeared, and in his letter there was much of that gnawing fear that seems to strike all men with the prison brand—a fear that a few of the peace officers and the public cruelly keep alive.

I am looking any day to have someone confront me with San Quentin [he said], and that is something I still have deeply in my heart and on my mind. I feel as though I had the weight of the world on my back. I would surely like to have an hour's talk with any lifer leaving there . . . I could tell him some things. I advise anyone coming out of there to throw all plans out the window, and take things as they find them. The world is certainly not as one dreams about it in there, and people on the outside are not nearly as interested in your welfare as the people on the inside are. I believe it comes as a shock to any man leaving there, if he will tell you the truth.

Wherever he is, John Hendricks at least knows that he left us a heritage of music that has done much to soften the gloom of prison, and the orchestra he inspired is now a permanent and useful fixture. As for the radio show, I look back on it as an important part of the experimental years in the new San Quentin, especially during the war, when the men needed confidence and public trust. I remember one blistering newspaper editorial which said: "They [the prisoners] would be a lot more useful to national defense if they had behaved like real men and were now able to fight instead of being caged up like mad dogs." The majority of the men, who had already tried everything short of a mass break to be released to the armed forces, were so stung and aroused by this kind of criticism that they literally demanded a chance to square themselves.

We took on enormous contracts for submarine nets, cafeteria trays, sirens, cargo slings, assault boats, and a hundred other items. We made thousands of night sticks for the State Guard, for instance—lethal clubs that would be useful to any escape-minded prisoner—without losing a single one.

While this war program was getting started, I was called to Washington for a conference with Maury Maverick, Warden Lawes, and others who were anxious to step up prison production. We went to the White House for one of those meetings, and while there I met Mrs. Franklin D. Roosevelt.

"Why don't you come and see us the next time you're in California?" I asked.

"I would be glad to," she said.

At the time I thought she was just being polite, and I really doubted that her incredibly busy schedule would permit a side trip to San Quentin. Some months later, when Mrs. Roosevelt was visiting her daughter in Seattle, her secretary called and asked if she could come down to the prison. Could she! I accepted the offer before Mrs. Roosevelt could change her mind, and met her at the main gate a week or so later. I had declared a half holiday for the men because I knew the inmates considered her visit a great honor, and piled them all into the mess hall to hear her talk. That speech was one of the most inspiring messages I have ever heard, and no man who was there that day will ever forget it. In some ways Eleanor Roosevelt's speech became San Quentin's secret weapon; it fired their pride and gave them the will to achieve miracles during the war.

And because Eleanor Roosevelt said so succinctly what I have been thinking and saying to the men for years, I want to quote here a small portion of that speech:

I am glad that I could come here today and see your work. Of course, not so very long ago, Mr. Maverick asked me if I would meet with a group of war production people and prison people to learn something about the production that was going on in the prisons. A little while after that meeting I went over to see what was being done in Baltimore. I had to get up very early and I didn't get to see the President, and the warden has asked me to tell you the little story of what happened.

As the President came out of his room to go to the office he called to my secretary, whose office is right near the elevator, "Where is my Mrs.?" My secretary called back, "She is in prison." Whereupon he answered, "I'm not surprised, but what's she in for?"

Now, more seriously, I want to tell you that I am thrilled by the work you are doing here because you seem to work fast and with a feeling of real urgency, and I have missed that in many factories. Sometimes when you go into a factory you feel the people are doing a good job but they aren't putting everything they have into it; I had the feeling today as I watched the men work that you were putting everything you have into it and you are getting re-sults. And I think what you have done in buying war bonds is perfectly remarkable, because the warden told me that that meant the sacrifice of your pleasures and your little luxuries, and I congratulate you all. It's worth it, because with all the faults we have in this country—and we have many—still this country is a wonderful country to live in. . . .

We have got to show that we can make our country meet the needs of the people, or we have nothing to offer the rest of the world; and the world has been through a terrible period of destruction and suffering. People all over the world have died, starved, and have undergone great cruelties; and when that happens you have to begin and build up again after you finally win. Even here in this country you are going to have men—and you are going to meet them in the future—who, because of their service in the war, are permanently handicapped. They are going to need helping hands . . . There are going to be so many boys losing an arm or a leg, with back injuries and all kinds of things that make a life harder to live. It isn't easy for you. I know that. You have a fight before you, but remem-ber that the war is going to make it hard for a great many men, and you perhaps can give a helping hand to men that are more handicapped than you will be.

When you do get a chance you will be living in com-munities; some of you will get your citizenship back. All of you will be neighbors to other people. Remember that you can only strengthen your country, and your country can only be as great as each community. And if we want to build peace, if we want to make our country a country in which there is less and less temptation for people to do wrong, a country in which we can make it harder for children to grow up under handicaps so that they do go wrong, then each one of us has a job to do in our community. And you can help because you know what is needed. You can talk to people who are the real leaders and who try to do the right thing for you and for their country. You can talk; you can make your neighbors understand. You can be a good citizen even before you vote again, and I think that is something that you must prepare for, somehow, during the war . . .

Prisoners know the meaning of liberty better than most men, and the inmates were so frantic to be doing something for their country that hundreds of them worked nights, Sundays, and holidays after finishing up their full eight-hour day for the state. Even then they weren't satisfied, and I had so many requests for more work that I was at my wit's end trying to line up new projects. Once, for example, I heard that the OPA was struggling with the problem of distributing eight million ration books in California. I phoned Francis Carroll, a San Francisco attorney who was OPA district director, and said we could handle the books at San Quentin.

"Well, Duffy," he said, "it's such a nervy idea that it must be good. We'll do it."

There was quite a discussion in the newspapers about our plan, some of it in a very skeptical vein, and I suspect that more than one official was shaky at the thought of two and a half billion dollars' worth of ration books—they were

valued at three hundred dollars apiece in the black market
—piled up in the state prison. But it never occurred to me
that anything could go wrong, and the men of San Quentin probably had their best laugh of the war the day the
books arrived. They had been kept in a San Francisco
warehouse under armed guard day and night. They were
delivered to us in armored trucks convoyed by a small
army of motorcycle police, and the citizens of the little San
Quentin village outside the gates must have thought we
were having a break. But after the policemen left I gave
the books to the inmates without a moment's hesitation,
and no free man touched them from then on. We finished
that prodigious addressing and mailing job in forty-three
days. We had been allowed a three per cent margin of
error, but when we were through, the OPA accountants
announced our errors were only one two-thousandth of
one per cent. Not a single ration book was lost.

Another time, when some righteous critic doubted
that the inmates could contribute much to the Third War
Loan drive, the men of San Quentin bought over one hundred thousand dollars' worth of war bonds of that issue—
one third the total sold in all American prisons. They were
allowed to "buy" a bomber, and for weeks there was an
excited discussion about a name for the plane. They suggested Jail Bird, Rock Buster, Pardon Me, Bars and Stripes,
Yegg Layer, and others, but finally settled on Bad Check—
because it would always come back. San Quentin's war-
bond purchases eventually totaled more than six hundred
thousand dollars, and I confess I don't know where they
got all the money. Only recently one man admitted, a little
sheepishly, that he had a "rich girl friend" and had per-

247

suaded her to buy twenty thousand dollars' worth of bonds through him at San Quentin. Another man—and this is a story that the men tell over and over—came to San Quentin for passing a fifty-dollar bad check in a Los Angeles bar. The bar owner, who had demanded a stiff sentence for our man, was arrested himself for subversive activities not long afterward and was sent to a federal prison with an additional penalty of deportation to Germany after the war. The San Quentin inmate, who had been working hard in a harvest camp so he could make restitution to the bar owner, doubled his working hours when he heard what had happened, and soon saved enough for a fifty-dollar bond. He mailed it to his victim at the other prison with a note that said: "When you arrive in Berlin there will be plenty of Americans who can cash this for you. Now we're square."

As the war progressed hundreds of San Quentin men were allowed to enlist on special service paroles authorized by the state legislature, and many were killed, wounded, or decorated for bravery. Those who stayed behind continued their zealous production activity, and it was a proud day when we were awarded the National Service Flag. Fifty per cent of all the men offered to give blood, too, and we had scores of members in the so-called "Gallon Club." Once, toward the end of the war, I got a letter from a man in a South Pacific hospital which said: "A buddy of mine was pretty badly shot up, and it took a lot of blood to keep him alive. I was there when the nurses opened up a case of blood marked 'San Quentin' and started pouring it into him. Well, Warden, I don't know whose blood it was, but it saved my pal's life and that's good enough for me." I read that letter to the men one day, and if some of them wept a little, you can be sure that all the others understood.

In many ways the war marked the coming of age of San Quentin. I knew, for example, that if we were to do our share of war production, we would need skilled machinists, welders, carpenters, toolmakers, and other craftsmen. Up to that time our school classes were held in the daytime and were limited to such fundamental subjects as reading, writing, and arithmetic under inmate teachers. One evening I attended a school board meeting at my old alma mater, the San Rafael High School, and pleaded with the members to assign some of their instructors for night classes at San Quentin. All the men on that board were my friends. They had known me for years, and I addressed them by their first names. But that evening they looked at me with incredulity.

"Night classes in San Quentin?" one of them said. "That seems like a risky thing. And I doubt if the taxpayers would like it if we used their money for teaching convicts."

I was numbed, which is putting it mildly. "The taxpayers should also know," I said, "that if a man isn't educated or trained while he is *in* prison, he will cost them a great deal more when he goes out and commits another crime because he still can't earn a living."

A few days later I drove over to Kentfield, a few miles away, and presented my plan to the board at the lively little College of Marin. They saw the validity of my arguments, realized that their own wartime enrollment was low, and agreed to give the idea a trial. We organized night classes immediately, unlocking the cells for hundreds of men and allowing them to go unescorted to the building we designated as our school. This system has been in effect ever since, with an average night enrollment of eighteen hundred men, and all our teachers, including some from my old school, are now certified and paid by the State Board of Education through these local school districts. It has certainly yielded dividends, and there is no more heart-warming sight for me than to attend one of our graduation ceremonies and watch scores of grown men, many of them middle-aged, receiving the grade-school diplomas they should have had years before. They go on from there, to our prison high-school or college courses, or they can learn a trade that will get them a job when they go free.

Today San Quentin—the once bloody battleground where brutality was the rule, and where guards like my father risked their lives every day for fifty dollars a month —is a huge, modern laboratory for the study of criminals and crime. Governor Earl Warren, aroused to our critical needs during the war, sponsored legislation which eventually created a California Department of Corrections. The new division, which covers all six of California's correctional institutions, is under the direction of Richard A. McGee, one of the ablest career penologists in the United States. His enthusiasm and understanding of prison life has meant a great deal to the wardens and superintendents whose complex and often critical problems he has to meet every day. In our own case we were able to start working on a bigger budget—San Quentin spent nearly four million dollars in 1948—which in turn brought better guard and personnel training, more security, a larger library, expanded educational and religious programs, badly needed new buildings and machinery, more work for the men, more forest camps, better food preparation, and many other improvements. Some years ago I tried to get a bill through the legislature that would permit paying the men up to fifty cents a day for their work, thus giving them a small stake for the parole day. Governor Warren ultimately signed such a measure, and the products the men manufacture for the state—such as furniture—have immeasurably reduced the cost of running the prison, while at the same time these factories are "making men."

Among other things, the new system under the Department of Corrections has made it possible to keep new arrivals separated from the other prisoners for an eight-week period in what is called the Guidance Center, while trained psychologists, sociologists, psychiatrists, religious advisers, and educators examine their crimes and the always long and tragic stories behind them, and plan their future with us. I was doing this sort of searching analysis on a small scale for years, trying to find clues to the mystery of crime, but our staff was never adequate. Even then, if I reached any conclusion at all, it was only that the majority of offenders had been juvenile delinquents at a very early age, came from poor or broken homes where little or no interest was shown in them, where discipline was lacking, and where they were allowed to quit school far too soon. Scientific analysis, of course, does not always reach the depths of a man's mind, or touch his heart. And if that fails, I like to think we can still remember the golden rule.

In that connection, I remember talking with a visiting professor one day when he asked me if I had majored in sociology at some university.

"No, I didn't," I said.

"Perhaps you're a psychologist," he said.

"No," I replied.

"Well," he persisted, "then you must be a penologist."

"I am not a sociologist, a psychologist, or a penologist," I said. "I guess I'm just a con-ologist."

Yes—the San Quentin of today is not the house of fear and forgotten men I knew in my youth. Much has been done; there is still much to do. We have removed almost all the outside tower guns, and our guards no longer carry clubs. Every inmate is assigned to a job. To eliminate idle time, which is a breeder of trouble, there are basketball, baseball, boxing, wrestling, and handball teams competing —and winning—against outside teams. Touch-tackle football has just been introduced—we have no turf for the regular game—for the first time in San Quentin's history. The men wear decent clothes, they go to school, they work, and they are in touch with the world. The ball-and-chain thug with his "dese" and "dose" remains in caricatures and cartoons, where he belongs, because the men in our Prison Town have their shoulders squared and as mature men their horizon has gone far beyond the high walls. They are in prison—and they don't forget it—but they know it is a prison with hope. They are not pampered, nor is their life soft and easy—but they know they are looked upon as human beings who will get a second chance in the outside world. Someday, I hope, there may be more prisons without walls and cells for most of those who have failed in their obligation to society. California's Department of Corrections already has such institutions, and soon there will be more. Meanwhile, though San Quentin still

252

has its towering blocks, its ten thousand locks, and its army of numbered men, I try to remember that it is the small things, the trivial pleasures and privileges, that make men keep up their fight to be decent human beings. I was thinking about this just the other day while I was in the visiting room watching a pretty young woman greet her imprisoned man. She had a tiny blond baby girl in her arms, and the man gazed at them both with the shadows of longing and loneliness in his eyes. He had been in San Quentin seven months, but his baby was only about four months old.

"I guess you've never held this baby, have you?" I asked.

"No, sir," he said in a whisper.

"Go ahead and take her," I said.

The guard near by looked at me incredulously; he knew it was against the rules. I nodded to him, and he said, "Well, Warden, if you say so, that's all I need." The man took the child and cradled her in his arms, and pressed his face against the soft little curls. He was silent for a long time, and the tears spilled down his cheeks. And then he smiled, and I knew he would do his time.

Yes—it was against the rules. But there are times when I would much rather break a rule than break a heart.